D1136242

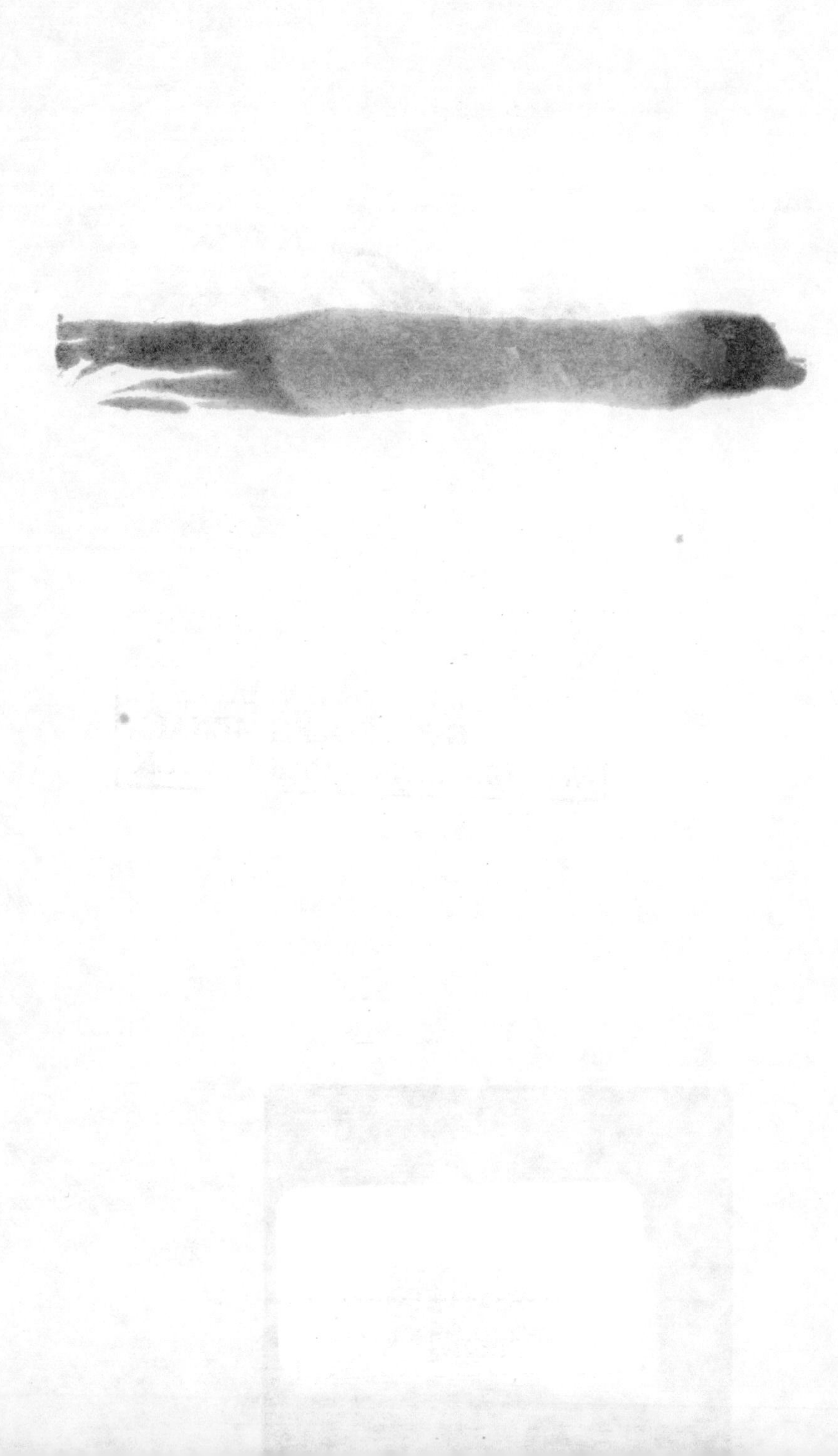

INTERESTING WAYS TO TEACH

53 INTERESTING WAYS TO ASSESS YOUR STUDENTS

In the same series

53 Interesting Things To Do In Your Lectures

53 Interesting Things To Do In Your Seminars And Tutorials

53 Interesting Ways Of Helping Your Students To Study

53 Interesting Communication Exercises For Science Students

53 Interesting Ways To Appraise Your Teaching

253 Ideas For Your Teaching

Interesting Ways To Teach: Seven 'Do-it-yourself' Training Exercises

and ...

Creating A Teaching Profile

53 Interesting Ways
To Assess Your Students

Graham Gibbs

Principal Lecturer and Educational Consultant

Oxford Polytechnic

Sue Habeshaw

Senior Lecturer and Course Advisor

Bristol Polytechnic

Trevor Habeshaw

Principal Lecturer (Educational Development)

Bristol Polytechnic

Published by

Technical & Educational Services Ltd

Printed by: Whitehall Printing Co. (Avon) Ltd.

First published in 1986 by
Technical and Educational Services Ltd
37 Ravenswood Road
Bristol BS6 6BW
Avon, U.K.

Second Edition 1988

ISBN 0 947885 11 0

Graham. Sue Trevor

Contents

Assessing Practical and Project Work (continued)

Preface

This book is addressed to teachers in further and higher education, though it is probably equally suitable for nurse tutors, YTS trainers, and others. Teachers in schools, too, will be able to adapt these ideas to their own situations.

The purpose of this book is to describe a wide range of ways of assessing students and to encourage teachers to extend the repertoire of assessment methods that they use. Variety is an important factor in effective assessment, as in effective teaching, and choice enables teachers to select those assessment methods which support their educational aims.

Though each item is written to make sense on its own, groups of items are gathered together under broader headings, and cross referenced, so that comparisons can easily be made. The methods range from the familiar standard essay to more technical areas such as computer based assessment and unconventional areas such as alternative exams.

Assessment is an aspect of education which, understandably, tends to raise student anxiety. When introducing a new method of assessment, you can help your students by telling them what it involves, explaining why you think it is worth doing and giving them time to think about it and discuss it.

This book is the third in the series Interesting Ways To Teach. The first two volumes are: **53 Interesting Things To Do In Your Lectures** and **53 Interesting Things To Do In Your Seminars And Tutorials**. The authors workshops in the methods described in the books, and full instructions for do-it-yourself training workshops are also obtainable from the publishers:

Technical and Educational Services Ltd
37 Ravenswood Road
BRISTOL
BS6 6BW

Graham Gibbs
Sue Habeshaw
Trevor Habeshaw

Glossary

Assessing

Assessing is a general term used to describe all those activities and processes involved in judging performance. Assessing can be summative or formative: summative assessment is concerned with a final judgement of performance; formative assessment is concerned with the improvement of performance. In broad terms **marking** and **grading** involve summative assessment while **reviewing** and **giving feedback** involve formative assessment.

Marking

Marking involves allocating scores to answers or student performances, and adding these to give a total score. Marking indicates how the performance relates to a maximum possible score: for example, 7 out of 10, or 70%.

Grading

Grading involves allocating a letter or symbol (eg. A,B,C,) to a performance. The letters usually have a special meaning in terms of the quality of performance they indicate, eg:

Grade	Honours Degree Classification
A	First Class
B+	Upper Second Class
B	Lower Second Class
C	Third Class
F	Fail

Reviewing

Reviewing involves making judgements, not about an individual piece of work or a specific performance, but about a wide range of abilities or achievements of a student at a particular time.

Giving Feedback

Giving feedback involves providing information for the student about the quality of her work or level of performance. While **marks** and **grades** provide some feedback, the term feedback is usually associated with more extensive qualitative information, such as that provided by written comments.

Evaluating

Evaluating involves judging teaching or courses rather than students, though assessing students can contribute to the evaluation of teaching and courses.

Essays

1 Standard Essay

2 Role Play Essay

3 Structured Essay

4 Interpretation of Evidence

5 Design

6 Note-Form Essays

7 Hypothesis Formation

Essay-type questions are probably used for coursework and final exams more frequently than any other type of assessment. There are characteristic problems, and advantages, associated with different types of essay question. Different types are suitable for assessing different aspects of student learning and different course objectives. In particular some types of question place a heavy emphasis on students' ability to write essays, to anticipate what questions will be asked and to guess what the questions mean. Such questions may be less effective in assessing students' understanding of what the teacher thinks is important. Awarding marks to conventional essays (**see 1 Standard Essay**) is a notoriously unreliable business, with differences between markers and differences between students' handwriting often having more effect on marks than the content of the essays. Also the very act of essay writing is very unlike the kinds of activities students are likely to engage in during their subsequent careers. Some of the ideas in this section (**see 3 Structured Essay**) can limit the undesirable side-effects of the use of essays, while others (**see 2 Role Play Essay**) can reduce the artificiality of the essay as a learning task.

Examples of each of the different types of question are given. One question, set in the context of the teaching of town planning, is used several times in different versions so as to illustrate the way a question can be developed to assess different objectives and channel students' efforts in different ways.

Standard Essay 1

This is the most common type of essay and may demand 1000 - 3000 word answers. Popular varieties include:

Quotation - Discuss (or Comment, or Query)

Q. "Land values are both a product and a determinant of the pattern of urban development." Discuss.

Q. Comment on the assertion that "although a good case can be made for free trade on the grounds of economic efficiency, there is no case on the grounds of equity".

Q. "Even after Locke's book was written the subject remained almost untouched and I fear that I will leave it pretty much as I found it" (Rousseau: the Preface to Emile). Did Rousseau leave education as he found it?

If the quotation is being used to encourage students to challenge expert opinion, this type of question can be helpful. If, however, its purpose is mainly decorative, then students will have problems working out what is important about the quotation. Obscure and invented quotations are likely to cause both students and markers considerable difficulties and confuse the issue as to what ability or knowledge is actually being assessed.

Write an essay on...

Q. Write an essay on fluid mechanics.

Q. Write an essay on language development in Down's Syndrome children up to 5 years.

Such questions run a variety of risks:

a the open-endedness makes it easy for students to cobble together enough disconnected facts and ideas to pass without revealing much thought or understanding;

b when they are used in examinations, students can revise and prepare complete answers on likely topics and trot them out without thought or reformulation;

c students can be stalled and panicked by the scope offered them;

d students may be being asked to produce an answer of a greater degree of generality than ever before;

e it isn't at all clear what would count as an acceptable answer.

Questions of this form may simply reveal their authors' inability to clarify their own teaching goals or their inablity to translate these into clear questions.

The potential advantage of such questions is the freedom it gives to students to choose what they will concentrate on and to structure their work themselves. This may allow excellent students to stand out more. However it may also give weaker students plenty of rope with which to hang themselves.

Describe, Give An Account Of, Compare, Contrast, Explain

Q. Describe how the Monte Carlo technique is used to shed light on the small sample properties of various estimation techniques.

Q. Give an account of the discovery and early use of penicillin.

Q. Compare and contrast the foreign policies of Disraeli and Gladstone.

Q. Explain the Phillips Curve and its applications.

Unlike "Assess..." questions, these questions do not explicitly require the student to express a viewpoint or conclusion. If there is such a requirement it should be clearly stated and the key issues specified, eg:

Q. Give an account of the discovery and early use of penicillin. What is your view of the scientific significance of this early work?

Q. Compare and contrast the foreign policies of Disraeli and Gladstone. Who was more successful, in your view, in protecting Britain's overseas interests? Justify your view with reference to events outside Europe.

Assess, Analyse, Evaluate

Q. Assess Richard as a strategist in the light of the expedition to Ireland in 1394.

Q. Analyse the difference between Locke's and Froebel's use of play in the education of young children.

Q. Evaluate the contribution of Japanese prints to the development of Impressionism.

These questions require not just information from the student, but a reasoned conclusion.

Trick Questions

Q. Is literalism a symptom of a dose of Flew?

Q. Can you do two things at once?

Q. Who, or what, unbound Prometheus?

While these questions may be very clever, they are probably only understood by the person who set them and her favourite three students. The first is from an English literature paper, the second from a cognitive psychology paper, and the third from an 18th century English history course and refers to the Industrial Revolution! Only those who attended all the lectures and the right seminars could have a clue what was being referred to. Trick questions are not recommended.

Role Play Essay 2

Q. You have inherited your late uncle's urban estate under his will and are considering whether it would be more profitable to sell the property quickly or 'sit and speculate'. Describe some of the factors you would consider in making your decision.

Q. Write a letter to the Minister of Education protesting about the lack of nursery school places in your county, giving economic arguments and emphasising evidence in government reports.

Q. Imagine you are a French journalist working for Le Monde. Write an article for the politics page about Britain's attitude towards trade in agricultural produce within the EEC, with specific reference to recent incidents involving French agricultural produce.

Such questions help students to see the relevance of the task and to take a personal interest in it. Their writing often becomes more natural and fluent. Even very small elements of simulation or role play can dramatically change students' approach to questions. There can be a danger of encouraging too flippant an approach but this can be kept in check by careful phrasing of the question, eg. write for The Times rather than the Sun; write to your member of parliament, not your grandmother.

This type of question is often used in law and accountancy with the instructions: "Advise your client....". The same kind of instructions can be given for any subject area, eg:

Q. Advise Weybridge Electrical Ltd. (by whom you have been hired as a consultant) on the suitability of the circuit designs in Appendix I given the performance specifications in Appendix II.

Q. Prepare a parliamentary answer for the Chancellor of the Exchequer (of whose think tank on the economy you are a prominent member) to the following tabled question concerning the recently published inflation figures: ....

Advise him on likely supplementary questions and on appropriate answers.

Structured Essay 3

Q. Identify and discuss some of the determinants of urban land values and their impact on urban development.
In your answer you should:

a define the following terms:
property rights in land,
zoning,
site value rating;

b explain the influence of these terms in determining land values;

c select one activity of public authorities, and one market factor, which affect land values and explain how each might influence urban development.

Q. Undertake a stylistic analysis of the following passage. Select, arrange and comment on features of syntax, lexis, semantics and (where relevant) phonology. Relate the artistic effects of the passage to the writer's choice of language.

By specifying the content in this way it is possible, when marking, to be clearer whether students know about and understand the specific things which you think matter. At the same time it becomes difficult to tell whether students would know which things matter without such prompting. You have to decide whether it is specific knowledge and techniques, or the ability to identify what matters, which is what you want to assess.

Questions can also be written in such a way that they specify the structure of the essay, eg:

Q. Is Heart of Darkness a Victorian novel?
Discuss the characteristic features of Victorian novels. Identify the key differences of post-Victorian novels. Highlight the main characteristics of Heart of Darkness. On the basis of the preceding three sections, draw conclusions about the extent to which Heart of Darkness is a Victorian novel.

Again you have to decide whether it is students' subject knowledge and analytical skills which you want to assess, or their ability to structure their own essays. If it is the former, then this type of question, by giving them a structure to use, will enable them to concentrate on content.

Interpretation of Evidence 4

Q. You own a house in a developing suburban area but are considering selling your property and moving closer to the city centre. Given the following demographic data:

....

....

what economic and social factors would you consider in coming to a decision?

Q. What light does the following experimental evidence throw on Triesman's model of selective attention?

....

....

Many standard essay questions (**see 1**) rely on students having undertaken analysis and interpretation at an earlier stage, eg. before an exam, and simply recalling these analyses in their answers. Interpretation questions require students to undertake this analysis 'live', and this can avoid regurgitation.

Design 5

Q. Design a new small shopping precinct for the site below........

To the above design brief can be added a requirement for the interpretation of evidence:

Q. Given the street plans, existing locations of shops, site values and other information in Appendices A-D, design and site a new small shopping precinct.

To this can be added elements of role play and structured questions:

Q. You are involved with the design of a new small shopping precinct. Given the street plans, existing locations of shops, site values and other information in Appendices A-D, draft an outline design for, and site, a new small shopping precinct which involves the demolition of an old street. Consider the possible effects on land value and accessibility of such a redevelopment and present an argument for such a siting to the planning officer.

This last version of the design question emphasises a quite different aspect of the design process and illustrates the way structured questions can focus on specific issues.

Design questions are common in architecture and town planning. They are not so common in a number of other subject areas where they are just as appropriate. For example in scientific and technical subjects the skills of experimental design are usually taught and assessed through teacher-designed experiments. It may not be until final-year undergraduate work, or even postgraduate work, that students design their own experiments. Even then less time tends to be spent on the design stage than on executing the design. Similarly in craft subjects, planning out how to undertake a complex task is often not tackled until late on in courses when all the component skills have been mastered.

It is easy to set design tasks (as in architecture) in order to develop the design skills required, even when the skills neccessary to implement the design have not yet been mastered, and there is no intention of implementing the design, eg:

Q. Design a method for establishing the frequency of occurrence of a particular microfossil in a sample of shale.

Q. Design an experiment to test the duration of short-term memory for verbal items following different kinds of initial information processing.

Note-Form Essays 6

Q. List the main economic factors which affect the pattern of changing land values. For each factor, itemise its limitations and potentialities for predicting future urban development. Your answer may be in note form.

Q. Briefly describe the significance for oil exploration of each of the following microfossil types:

....

....

etc.

This type of question is used most often to assess the recall of key items of information or test simple understanding of terms, formulae, apparatus, tools and so on. It is less suitable for assessing analysis, synthesis of ideas, creativity and so on. Sometimes note-form questions are used to assess whether students understand what is significant about a topic, eg:

Q. Write notes on two of the following:

a ....

b ....

c ....

d ....

Students who have plenty to say about the topics and are obliged to select the main points are faced with the problem of guessing which aspects the marker thinks are most important. Poor students can gain marks by writing down whatever comes into their heads about any of the topics, and this may be why this form of question is so common: to avoid having to fail very poor students. Note-form essays are also easier and quicker (though less interesting) to mark.

Hypothesis Formation 7

Q. Suggest the relationship between nearby house prices and:

a the development of a new shopping precinct in a suburban area;

b a road-widening scheme in the same area.

Hypothesis formation questions can be combined with data interpretation to encourage students to be speculative in their analyses:

Q. Speculate as to the possible causes of the data trends in the table below....

or linked to design questions to encourage self-criticism or reflection. For example the question developed in item 5 above ("Design a new small shopping precinct for the site below............") could be expanded by the addition of the question:

Q. Speculate as to the likely planning objections raised to your plans by:

a the local community;

b the planning officer.

Objective Tests

8 Right/Wrong

9 Short Answer

10 Completion

11 True/False

12 Matching

13 Multiple Choice

14 Multiple Completion

15 Assertion/Reason

16 Best Answer

Objective tests are simply tests which produce student answers (or responses, or actions, or products) which can be marked objectively. With an objective test it is clear what the criteria are for marking, and these criteria can be used reliably with no scope for idiosyncratic, personal or subjective judgement. An essay is not an objective test because its requirements cannot be specified sufficiently clearly to allow objective marking. Requiring someone to clear five feet in the high jump is an objective test: everyone would agree whether or not the person had failed the jump. Simple factual tests are also usually objective tests. For example marking answers to the question "What is the capital of Canada?" involves little in the way of subjective judgement (except perhaps in the matter of spelling mistakes, and even these judgements could be made objective by specifying in advance which spelling mistakes would be tolerated).

The main potential advantages of objective tests are:

a improved reliability: different markers could agree on a mark, and the mark would be a good indicator of what a student could do;

b ease and speed of marking: this is especially the case when students indicate their answers by ticking possible alternatives as in the case of multiple choice questions.

Computers can be used to mark some forms of objective test (**see 22 Computer Marking**).

The main disadvantages of objective tests are:

a trivialisation of learning: it is often the case that only low level abilities are assessed by objective tests. The adoption of objective testing can result in a narrowing of the curriculum to what can be easily tested in this way. In fact high level abilities can be assesed by objective tests though this requires more imagination from the test designer. It is the poor use of objective tests which gives them a bad name rather than the intrinsic nature of the tests;

b lack of feedback: if students get an objective test item wrong then they may well want to know why. Most forms of objective test (though not all) provide them with no feedback on their learning.

Neither of the disadvantages is insurmountable. The solution is to get the advantages of objective tests without also having the disadvantages.

This section contains examples of the main types of objective test. Some of these examples have design errors in order to illustrate how <u>not</u> to write objective tests, and these are followed by notes explaining the error.

Right/Wrong 8

Q. Which Indian tribe fought in the Battle of Little Big Horn?

Such right/wrong questions can also be used to test problem solving and arithmetical manipulation - or in the case of the question below even the use of a slide rule or set of mathematical tables:

Q. What is the square root of 169?

Short Answer 9

Q. What were the three recommendations of the Trevelyan Report of 1854?

1...

2...

3...

It can be helpful to indicate the length of answer required by use of dotted lines or spaces in the layout.

Completion 10

Q. The Battle of Little Big Horn was fought by ....

The problem with this question is that a variety of answers could be correct, eg. Custer, Sioux, Indians, American Cavalry etc. If you start providing cues to avoid unwanted answers (eg. "S---x") the questions can become both too easy and a test of recognition memory rather than of recall. It is often better to use a simple right/wrong question (**see 8**).

True/False 11

Q. The First Lord of the Treasury is the Chancellor of the Exchequer. TRUE / FALSE

True/false questions are open to guessing. Random choice would score 50% and sensible guessing more than 50%. A simple guessing correction can be made by subtracting the number of questions answered incorrectly from the total answered correctly to give the score.

The above question requires the student to remember facts, and factual recall is the most common demand made by these simple forms of objective test item. There are also, however, quite complex analyses, calculations, derivations etc. which have clearly right or wrong answers and which lend themselves to questions of the right/wrong, short answer, or true/false type. For example:

Q. Given the above case study and data, which of the following statements about the situation are true?

1. ".." TRUE / FALSE
2. ".." TRUE / FALSE
3. etc. TRUE / FALSE

Matching 12

Q. Match each of the items in LIST X with one of the dates in LIST Y by filling in the boxes below the lists. Do not use any of the boxes in LIST Y more than once.

LIST X

1. County Borough Councils set up
2. Urban District Councils set up
3. County Councils set up
4. Educational duties transferred from School Boards to Councils
5. Powers of Boards of Guardians transferred to Councils.

LIST Y

A 1894
B 1895
C 1902
D 1929
E 1888
F 1835

LIST X	1	2	3	4	5
LIST Y					

There are more items in LIST Y than in LIST X to avoid the fifth answer being identified by elimination. Also the logic of this question (Councils have to be set up before powers can be transferred to them!) will make it easier for students to get the answers right.

Matching type questions can also be used to test comprehension, eg:

Q. For each item in Column 1 select the criticism in Column 2 which is most appropriate to it. Record your answer in the box preceding the question number. Do not use items from Column 2 more than once.

Column 1

1. Multiple Choice
2. True/False
3. Matching
4. Essay
5. Short Answer

Column 2

A. It tends to result in extensive sampling of comprehension in a limited number of content areas.
B. It should be used primarily for measuring comprehension.
C. Judgement of scorers influences test reliability.
D. The items must be relatively easy to be meaningful.
E. To write good items requires skill and time.
F. It cannot measure creativity.

The student is likely to tackle such a question by reading an item from column 1 and then reading through all the items in column 2 in order to find a matching item. It would save the student time if the columns were reversed so that the repeated reading is of the briefer items. This type of question, which requires the most appropriate alternative to be selected, is known as "best answer" (**see 16**).

Multiple Choice 13

Q. A customs tax is imposed on Japanese toys imported into the United Kingdom in order to give direct assistance to:

A	UK importers
B	UK exporters
C	Japanese toymakers
D	UK toymakers
E	Maximise free trade

The grammatical difference in alternative E excludes it from consideration. It would be better to use another item more similar to items A - D (eg. 'Japanese exporters') to provide a better 'distractor', or feasible wrong answer.

The key to writing good multiple choice questions lies in devising good distractors. The standard of distractors is often low, and this has led to the publication of booklets which advise students how to answer multiple choice questions when they don't know the answer. At Minnesota University there are even study skills courses, for which students gain course credits, which teach this skill.

Multiple choice questions can be used to test analysis, calculations, interpretation etc. by providing initial evidence or data to which the question refers, eg:

Q. Given the following series of shoe sizes:

4, 4, 4, 5, 6, 9, 10,

Which number gives the median?

A 4
B 5
C 6
D 9
E 10

Which number gives the mode?

A 4
B 5
C 6
D 9
E 10

Multiple choice questions are possible to answer by guessing: in the examples above the student has a 20% chance of getting the answer correct without any knowledge of statistics. If there were only three options then this likelihood would rise to 33%. As a consequence, multiple choice questions tend not to have less than four options. However, more than five options may lead to confusion and so most, in practice, have five. Test scores will still need to be adjusted to compensate for the effects of guessing.

Multiple Completion 14

Q. The assets of a commercial bank can be set out in the following categories:

1 Investments
2 Bills discounted
3 Money at call and short notice
4 Advances
5 Cash in hand and at the Bank of England

Which of the following combinations of the above assets form the liquidity ratio?

A 1, 2 and 3
B 2 and 3
C 2, 3 and 4
D 2, 3 and 5
E 3, 4 and 5

Multiple completion questions are simply multiple choice questions in which several of the alternatives together constitute the correct answer.

Poor multiple completion questions can be more open to guessing than multiple choice questions. In the question above answer A seems unlikely because it is the only alternative containing option 1, and answer B seems unlikely because it is the only alternative which contains only two options. The chance of getting this question right by guessing is therefore increased from 20% to 33%.

Multiple completion questions can assess more complex skills than can multiple choice questions. However the complexity can also confuse the student and complex-looking questions sometimes obscure the fact that only very low level objectives are being tested.

Assertion/Reason 15

Q.	ASSERTION	REASON
	The monarch rules Britain	The law assumes that the monarch can do no wrong

In this form of objective test the question is set out in the form of an assertion or statement, and a reason or explanation of it. The student must decide whether the assertion and reason are correct statements, and whether the reason adequately explains the assertion. The following coding scheme is used to enable the student to make a simple response:

A The assertion and reason are correct statements AND the reason correctly explains the assertion.

B The assertion and reason are correct statements BUT the reason does not explain the assertion.

C The assertion is correct BUT the reason is incorrect.

D The assertion is incorrect BUT the reason is correct.

E BOTH the assertion and reason are incorrect.

(The answer to this question is D because although the reason, on its own, is correct, the assertion is not.)

This format looks complex and confusing at first, but with familiarity it can be used to test reasoning as well as recall and comprehension. It can be used in conjunction with a case study, experimental evidence, data etc. to test students' interpretation of the evidence, as in the next question.

Q. Given the above statistics concerning law and order, and crimes committed between 1950 and 1980, code each of the following pairs of statements and explanations, using the A - E answer codes given above:

ANSWER CODE		STATEMENT	EXPLANATION
	1.	Murders increased between 1970 and 1980.	There were fewer Police per 1000 of the population.
	2.	etc............	

Best Answer 16

Q. A manual for an aptitude test reports a Kuder-Richardson reliability of +0.95 for 25,000 children. Which of the following conclusions about the test is most appropriate?

A	It is highly reliable
B	It is highly valid
C	It is highly internally consistent
D	It is suitable for selection purposes

Best answer questions tend to be more difficult than other types of objective test. They involve finer discriminations and wrong answers are not so obviously wrong that they are easy to eliminate. Best answer questions can be useful when an understanding or interpretation of information is required and can be used following data or case studies.

A problem in devising best answer questions is that the correct answer has to be sufficiently better as an answer than the alternatives to avoid argument or unfairness, but not so much better that it is obvious. However it is usually easier to devise correct but poor answers as distractors for best answer questions than it is to devise incorrect answers which are effective as distractors for standard multiple choice questions.

Alternative Exams

Seen Exam 17

A curse of conventional unseen exams is the extent to which students simply memorise selected information in the hope that it will be relevant to the questions which turn up, and then regurgitate this information wherever they can fit it in. Even sensible exam questions do not entirely avoid this problem. Such exams are very hit and miss affairs with some students guessing correctly what will come up and others being unlucky and memorising the wrong selection of material. In the exam itself students can be more concerned to use what they have memorised than to answer the questions appropriately. Students under extreme time pressure place a higher priority on 'getting it all down' than on organising their answers and so regurgitate all over the place. Exam answers look terrible and are a very poor reflection of the quality of work of which the students are capable. Furthermore students forget much of what they have mugged up for an exam - usually within a few weeks - because of the ways they have prepared for the exam. Memorising by rote has very short term consequences for learning.

Teachers tend to tolerate this situation in order to be able to 'sample' student learning. They assume that, if they unpredictably test a small number of elements from a course, the students' exam performance will be a reliable indicator of what they have learnt across the whole course (it being impossible to assess everything). The practical
consequences seem a high price to pay for this dubious assumption.

Some of the negative consequences of unseen exams can be avoided by using seen exams. If you show students your exam paper at the start of a course there are both positive and negative effects.

Positive effects

a Students are very clear about what the real demands of the course are: what is to be learnt and what is peripheral.

b Students' exam answers are of a much higher quality.

c The element of luck is eliminated.

d What distinguishes good answers from bad tends to be how much work students have done and how much they understand.

e Students are less anxious about the exam.

f Students can be involved in setting exam questions.

Negative effects

a Students may orient themselves narrowly to the exam questions and take unexamined topics less seriously during the course.

b Students can still memorise whole answers. The exam can become an exercise in writing out from memory an answer prepared some time before.

c Students are still under time pressure in the exam itself.

d Students can cheat by obtaining help to prepare for the exam.

The first of these negative effects can be minimised either by setting broad and theoretical questions which have no right answers and which require considerable thought rather than mere reproduction. Even if a worked through answer is subsequently memorised to be written out in the exam, this may not matter much provided that the original learning has been undertaken. In this case, however, there seems little point in having an exam rather than coursework or an extended exam (**see 18 168-Hour Exam**). Alternatively it is possible to select the final exam questions from a wider range shown at the start of the course (**see 19 Revealed Exam Questions**).

The second and third of these negative consequences can be eliminated by extending the time period allowed to complete the exam and by allowing access to resources so that memorising is not necessary (**see 20 Open Book Exam**).

The 168-Hour Exam 18

Conventional three-hour unseen exams, with no access to books, notes or other resources, are a rather curious way of testing ability. Students will probably never face the same kind of test of memory under such extreme time pressure in any subsequent work. It is perhaps because conventional exams bear so little relation to the world of work that degree results are such a poor predictor of subsequent success in careers. Exams even bear little resemblance to what independent postgraduate research looks like. A more realistic way of testing students would assess their ability to research, redraft and use resources and would place less emphasis on 'sprinting ability'. It would also avoid the element of luck involved in conventional exams (**see 17 Seen Exam**).

The 168-hour exam simply involves allowing students one week between receiving the exam paper and submitting their answers. During this week they can use their notes, the library and other resources. They may even be permitted to use their colleagues and their teachers - though this can lead to problems. In a sense it is simply an important end-of-course assignment with a one-week time limit.

<u>Advantages of this kind of exam include:</u>

- a the elimination of memorising and question-spotting;
- b a considerable reduction in anxiety before the exam;
- c much higher quality answers;
- d the testing of something more worthwhile;

e the encouragement to students to keep thorough and useful notes during the course.

Disadvantages of this kind of exam include:

a high levels of student anxiety during the exam week, and excessive study hours (though probably no more than revision hours for a conventional exam);

b disruption of other courses or exams: it is unreasonable to expect students to do much else during a week-long exam;

c great student competition for library books, or even the hiding of library books. This can be minimised by the placing of crucial books on very short term loan. It can also force students to purchase their own books;

d increased likelihood of cheating: students are able to get outside help. This is a risk with all assessed coursework, however, and can be checked by using a viva (**see 29**).

Revealed Exam Questions 19

Last year's exam paper often provides students with the best guide as to what the course is really about and which learning outcomes are the most important in terms of assessment. An excellent way to inform students about what really mattered on this year's course would be to show them this year's exam paper at the start of the year.

The obvious problem is that students would be likely to select a few of the questions (if the exam is of the common "Answer three out of eight" format) and restrict themselves to these topics, ignoring the rest of the course material. A way around this is to devise an exam paper with a broad question on each of the major topics and to tell students at the start of the year:

> "These are the exam questions. However the exam paper will only contain three of them and you will have to answer all three."

In this way students are obliged to study every area of the course but without the handicap of not knowing what is going to be asked about each area. Revision is less of an anxious hit and miss affair and student effort is more focussed.

Conventional exam papers seldom give students no choice because this might be considered unfair and might in any case lead to a high failure rate! But as soon as you provide choice you encourage students to miss out parts of the course in order to concentrate on what they think is likely to come up in the exam. Choice also allows students to cover up their weaknesses and gives a distorted impression of their knowledge of the whole course. Revealed exam questions give less encouragement to selective negligence. While question spotting is still possible, it is much more risky. Such questions therefore provide a more accurate indication of students' all-round knowledge.

Open Book Exam 20

A common criticism of conventional exams is that they test memory rather than anything more important, such as the ability to analyse or criticise. In practice professionals do not rely heavily on memory for information: they keep key textbooks and reference sources at hand and consult them as and when they need to. They have to be familiar with these sources, but they probably don't need to memorise much of their contents. It does not seem sensible to deny students access to what are everyday tools of the trade. Indeed the skills required to use these tools quickly and effectively may themselves be worth assessing.

In some subjects it would be ludicrous to prevent student access to key reference sources : for example to refuse the use of astronomical tables to students of navigation. In other subject areas such as English literature it has become common for key texts to be available during the exam because students are being tested on what they can say about the texts, not what they can remember or quote from memory. At the National Technical Highschool in Bergen, in Norway, the engineering students have access to terminals linked to the main frame computer during their one-day final exams, and access to any computer programs they like, including programs or information they have previously entered themselves. So the solving of complex engineering problems in the exam more closely simulates the way working engineers operate. If a student has written special programs to tackle particular types of problem and knows how to use these programs, then good luck to her! There seems to be much more scope for open book exams than is usually exploited.

The main objections to open book exams come from courses where students are being tested on their memory for facts, definitions or algorithmic procedures, all of which are readily available in textbooks. In such cases the availability of books would largely invalidate the exam - but then one might question the value of such exams in the first place.

Providing reference sources which contain data can allow much more complex questions to be set for students than in conventional exams (**see 4 Interpretation of Evidence**). Open book exams also encourage students to become thoroughly conversant with selected texts and even to buy their own copies!

'Doing It' Exam 21

Very often the real objectives of a course are not well matched by the kind of assessment used. In particular, courses with mainly practical aims are often assessed by end-of-course exams using standard essay questions (**see 1**). To illustrate this point we will examine an introductory course in history in a polytechnic. This course ran in the first term of the first year of a three-year degree programme. The course was designed to introduce alternative theoretical perspectives on social change so that in subsequent courses, which were mainly set in the context of particular periods and locations, students would be able to examine historians' evidence and explanations of evidence with an awareness of the theoretical perspectives of the writers.

The exam questions, however, were of the form:

> "Compare and contrast the theories of Condorcet and de Bonald".

Because they came from an 'A'-level history background where they were expected to memorise material, students interpreted such questions as requiring them to memorise and list the main features of the theorists. Their exam answers revealed little about their ability to recognise theoretical assumptions in the writings of historians, and the nature of the exam did little to encourage the development of this skill during the course.

To turn this exam into a 'Doing It' exam would require, for example, the selection of a recent history journal article, and the instruction to students:

> "Read this article and comment on the theoretical perspective of

the author with particular reference to her interpretation of the evidence she presents".

This kind of task would both test what the course was trying to achieve and orient students' efforts during the course towards the course goals rather than towards memorising.

A gap between theoretical underpinnings and the practical goals of courses is often evident in education courses. Final exams commonly contain standard essay questions on the main theories of the psychology, sociology and philosophy of education. One course for further education lecturers replaced such essay questions with a 'Doing It' exam. The students were shown a videotape of a further education lecturer teaching a class. They were then asked a series of practical questions about her performance which reflected psychological, sociological and philosophical issues. They were also asked to advise the lecturer on the future conduct of her teaching. One of the main aims of the course was that students should become more sophisticated in their ability to analyse practical teaching and see ways to improve it. This new exam tested exactly that.

In law, 'Doing It' exams can be based upon analysing cases or advising clients rather than simply upon recalling legal principles or precedents.

In science, 'Doing It' exams can be based upon interpreting data or reading and commenting on a journal article describing experimental work, rather than upon recall of definitions, formulae or mathematical procedures.

'Doing It' exams can be extended over time if conventional two or three hour exam slots artificially constrain the nature of the 'doing' element (**see 18 The**

168-Hour Exam).

Computer Based Assessment

Computer Marking 22

Most of the types of test item in the section on objective tests (**see11 - 16**) require students simply to make a mark in a box to indicate their answer. It can be very tedious and time consuming to identify which marks are in the right place, how many of them there are, and so on. There are now a number of computer-based devices which can read and record such marks for you.

The simplest devices involve a cheap 'reader' which can recognise graphite on specially printed cards. Students use a soft pencil and answer questions by making their marks on the kind of card reproduced below.

NAME

COURSE

STUDENT NUMBER

	0	1	2	3	4	5	6	7	8	9
	0	1	2	3	4	5	6	7	8	9
	0	1	2	3	4	5	6	7	8	9
	0	1	2	3	4	5	6	7	8	9
	0	1	2	3	4	5	6	7	8	9

ANSWERS

1	A	B	C	D	E	2	A	B	C	D	E
3	A	B	C	D	E	4	A	B	C	D	E
5	A	B	C	D	E	6	A	B	C	D	E
7	A	B	C	D	E	8	A	B	C	D	E
9	A	B	C	D	E	10	A	B	C	D	E
11	A	B	C	D	E	12	A	B	C	D	E
13	A	B	C	D	E	14	A	B	C	D	E
15	A	B	C	D	E	16	A	B	C	D	E
17	A	B	C	D	E	18	A	B	C	D	E
19	A	B	C	D	E	20	A	B	C	D	E
21	A	B	C	D	E	22	A	B	C	D	E
23	A	B	C	D	E	24	A	B	C	D	E
25	A	B	C	D	E	26	A	B	C	D	E
27	A	B	C	D	E	28	A	B	C	D	E

This kind of card allows the recording of the student's name, number, and course and responses to 100 five-alternative questions. The cards are fed through the reader (a box the size of a dictionary) by hand. A simple program on a personal computer will then store and collate data. Such programs often give total scores for each student on request and a breakdown of responses to each question (to show which questions are too easy or hard and which do not contribute to the overall score).

Notes :

a A system like this could cost as little as £1,000 (1986 prices) for a microcomputer, a reader, a printer to print out the results, the software and other minor bits and pieces you'd need.

b If you already have access to a microcomputer (eg. an Apple IIe or a BBC B) and printer, then a card reader and software could cost around £300. A reader which could recognise any kind of mark (for example ball-point, rather than only graphite pencil) would cost around £800.

c The cards for these cheap systems are relatively expensive, though they can be used repeatedly until all 100 spaces are used up. Your print room could produce them more cheaply provided that they can print the magnetic ink alignment marks down the left hand side with sufficient accuracy.

d Graphite readers can be unreliable in that unless bold marks are produced from a soft pencil, they may not be consistently recognised.

e Matching up the reader to your own microcomputer and adapting standard software can pose niggling problems. However you could write your own software if you have even limited skills in using BASIC.

f More sophisticated systems can recognise any sort of mark very reliably on a wide variety of plain paper form layouts. They can be programmed to read a variety of different forms, have automatic form-feeders which operate at high speed and have various data-analysis software built in. If you can afford such a system it would be much easier, faster, and more reliable to use. It would also allow a range of question formats which the simple systems cannot cope with. It would cost £4,000 - £10,000 (1986 prices) depending on its facilities. An example of a form for such a reader is reproduced on page 70.

Sheet

[0] [1] [2] [3] [4] [5] [6] [7] [8] [9]

BIOGRAPHICAL QUESTIONNAIRE

Surname: | | | | | | | | | | | | | | | | | | | | **Initials:** | | | **Employee Number:** | | | | | | | |

Please remember:
- Mark the boxes in pencil.
- Rub out mistakes thoroughly.
- Mark the boxes like ▬ not like [/]. Fill them completely.
- Do not fold the questionnaire.
- Make no marks outside the questionnaire.

CLASSIFICATION DETAILS

1. How old were you when you joined

Less than 16 ▭ 16 - 17 ▭ 18 - 19 ▭ 20 - 21 ▭ Over 21 ▭

2. What was your highest educational qualification at the time you joined? (Do not include examinations passed after joining).

No formal qualifications ▭
CSE, RSA, School Cert ▭
'O' levels, ONC, OND ▭
Highers, 'A' levels, HNC, HND ▭
University Degree ▭

EARLY LIFE AND FAMILY

3. Please compare the number of years you have spent in full-time education with the corresponding period spent by your parents. Have you spent . . .?

More than either parent ▭
More time than one parent ▭
About the same amount of time as both ▭
Less time than both parents ▭

4. In how many different and separate locations – towns, villages, etc – had you lived up to the time you left school?

One only ▭ 2 to 3 ▭ 4 to 5 ▭ 6 or more ▭

5. What is your position in your family?

First born ▭
Second born ▭
Third or later child ▭

6. What is the gap in age between yourself and your nearest brother or sister?

Less than 2 years ▭
2 to 5 years ▭
More than 5 years ▭
Does not apply ▭

7. How important were each of these factors in the household in which you grew up? (Mark your answer by marking one box in each row).

	Not Important	Important	Very Important
Firm discipline	▭	▭	▭
Getting on well at school	▭	▭	▭
Fitting in with the rest of the family	▭	▭	▭
Joining in lots of outside activities	▭	▭	▭
Music, Art, Theatre	▭	▭	▭
Travel	▭	▭	▭

8. How was the household in which you grew up organised? (Please mark one only, choosing the best description.)

Everyone had set tasks/responsibilities ▭
We all helped with the regular domestic chores, but not on an organised basis ▭
Household jobs were done entirely by my parent(s) ▭
Cannot recall ▭

SCHOOL

9. How many different schools did you attend between the ages of 11 and 18?

One only ▭ 2 or 3 ▭ 4 or more ▭

10. Think of the secondary school you attended for longest, between the ages of 11 and 18. Was it . . .? (Please answer one in each row)

a) Single sex? ▭ Mixed? ▭
b) Private? ▭ State-funded? ▭
c) Denominational or run by a religious order? Yes ▭ No ▭
d) Selective entry? ▭ Comprehensive? ▭
e) Boarding School* ▭ Day-School? ▭
(*note: mark only if you boarded)

11. How old were you when you left secondary education?

Under 16 ▭ 16 ▭ 17 ▭ 18 ▭ 19 or over ▭

12. Did you ever win prizes for academic achievement while at secondary school?

No, never ▭ Yes, once ▭ Yes, several times ▭ School(s) did not award prizes ▭

13. Did you hold a position of exceptional responsibility at your secondary school (eg. Head Pupil, House Captain)?

No ▭ Yes ▭ No such positions at my school ▭

Computer Generated Test Papers 23

Sometimes it is necessary to have alternative versions of a test paper of equal difficulty: for resits, for subsequent years, to prevent students from helping each other (should that be considered undesirable), and so on. With some forms of objective test item it is a very simple matter to produce alternative versions of an item with only minor changes of wording or content, eg:

Q. A1 Give the electronic configuration of the following ions:

Fe(II) Cu(II) Ni(II)

or

A2 Give the electronic configuration of the following ions:

Fe(III) Ti(III) Ni(III)

Q. B1 Draw the orbitals:

dyz dxz

or

B2 Draw the orbitals:

dxz dxz - yz

These alternative items for each topic can then be typed into a file in a computer:

TOPIC AREA	A	B	C	D	etc.
ITEM	A1	B1	C1	D1	etc.
	A2	B2	C2	D2	etc.
	A3	B3	C3	D3	etc.
	A4	etc	....	....	....

A simple programme will randomly select one item from topic area A, one from topic area B, and so on, and print out the resulting list of items. In this way a unique test paper can be printed for each student.

Computer Generated Problems

24

In most science and technology subjects students are required to do problems involving calculations with answers which are either right or wrong. Usually the teacher demonstrates how to do a particular kind of problem and then sets the students a couple of examples to try for themselves. A difficulty for the teacher is that there is a limit to the number of problems which it is practical to set: it simply takes too long to devise a large number of comparable problems and to calculate the correct numerical answers in order to be able to mark students' work. Individual students don't get as much practice as might be desirable, and it becomes very easy for students to collaborate or cheat because they are all tackling the same problems and can easily check their answers with each other.

It is relatively easy to produce a computer program which generates unique problems, allowing students to get as much practice as they need, preventing unwanted collaboration, and calculating correct answers to aid marking.

One version of such a programme has the following components:

a a file containing the names of the students in the class for whom problems are to be generated;

b a question in a specified format;

c an algorithm for calculating the correct answer from the variables in the question;

d a file containing a set of permissible values for each variable;

e a teacher's file in which are stored the values generated for each of the variables for each student, and the answer to each problem, calculated from the algorithm.

The questions can be of the form (the variables are underlined):

Q. If <u>six</u> <u>20 horsepower</u> pumps can empty <u>three</u> <u>10,000 ton</u> oil tankers in <u>24 hours</u> how long will it take to empty <u>two</u> <u>8,000 ton</u> tankers with <u>four</u> <u>30 horsepower</u> pumps?

There are 4 variables in this question, and if 5 permissible values were input for each variable it would be possible to generate $5^4 = 625$ unique problems by randomly selecting one of the permissible values for each of the variables. The programme will print out a sheet for each student with the student's name on it and a unique problem, and will record on a file for the teacher the values involved (in this case: 6, 20, 3, 10,000, 24, 2, 8,000, 4, and 30) and the correct answer, calculated with the algorithm. Marking then simply involves checking students' answers against those in the teacher's file. Automatic marking could be added to this programme (**see 22 Computer Marking**) and tutorial comments for incorrect answers could be given automatically by inserting the student's unique values for the variables into a standard explanation of how to do the calculation (**see 25 Computer Feedback to Students**).

Words or letter strings can be substituted for numerical data as variables in questions, to allow the use of this question generator in subject areas not involving numerical calculations. However this is likely to be more difficult than for numerical applications.

Once the program has been written, you only need to specify the question format, the algorithm, and the names of the students, to be able to generate as many problems as you like, together with their answers.

Computer Feedback to Students 25

With computer-marked multiple choice questions the only feedback students usually get is a score for the number of correct answers. Even in the Open University, which pioneered the widescale use of computer marked tests and undertakes very sophisticated analysis and development of the tests themselves, until recently all the students were told about their assignment was the grade they had been given (ie. A, B, C etc). They had no way of knowing which questions they got wrong, or why.

As feedback is so important to learning it is worth thinking about about how to provide feedback even within a computer-based assessment system. The system described here is known as T.I.P.S. (Teaching Information Processing System). This is a system developed at Duke University, U.S.A., and adapted for the assessment of economics students at Heriot Watt University, Edinburgh, and of science students at Ulster Polytechnic.

When writing the test items, the author also writes a tutorial comment which would provide the basis for answering the item correctly. When the computer marks a student's responses to multiple choice questions it also prints out a total score, and the tutorial comments for the questions which the student answered incorrectly,eg:

"Student Progress Report

Student A.N.Other

Survey No. 1

Biochemistry Test No. 3

You correctly answered 23 out of the 25 questions in this survey.

Amides are generally neutral. The carbonyl removes the basic properties from the adjacent -NH2 or -NHR.

Oxidation of a mercapton (thiol), RSH, causes two molecules to link to give a disulphide RSSR and water is eliminated."

Reference

J.D. Ruddick (1985) "The use of T.I.P.S. with physiotherapy students" in Gibbs G. (Ed), Alternatives in Assessment 2: Objective Tests and Computer Applications , Standing Conference on Educational Development Services in Polytechnics, Occasional Paper 21, Birmingham.

Computer Based Keller Plan 26

The Keller Plan is a method for structuring courses, also known as P.S.I. (Personalised System of Instruction). In it the course content is divided up into units, commonly about a week in length. Full sets of objectives are written for each unit, in the form: "At the end of this unit you will be able to: ....". Objective tests (**see 8-16**) are written for each unit to test whether students have achieved the objectives for that unit. Students have to pass these tests before being allowed to continue to the next unit, and the pass mark is set very high: mastery is the goal. Students work at their own pace using whatever resources are available to them. Usually Keller Plan courses are resource-based, rather than dependent on the classroom or teacher, which allows greater flexibility of scheduling.

When a student judges herself to be ready, she takes the test for the unit she has been studying. If she passes the test, then she is given the objectives for the next unit and can continue. If she fails, she is given individual tuition on the questions she answered incorrectly, and given the opportunity to resit a similar test. Several parallel forms of the test are available to allow repeated resits. The main involvement of the teacher (once the course units and tests have been designed) is in the testing and tuition, and it is here that the computer can be used.

Objective tests can be set up on the computer. When the student feels ready, she can sit at a terminal or micro and call up the appropriate test. If she gets enough of the questions right then the objectives to the next unit are displayed and can be printed out, and the student can start working towards them.

<u>Possible additions to this basic format</u> :

a Alternative forms of each test (or test item) can be held in the computer and randomly selected for use with each student, to avoid students informing each other about test questions, and to allow new tests to be presented for resits. Ideally unique questions or tests would be generated (**see 23 Computer Generated Test Papers and 24 Computer Generated Problems**).

b Tutorial comments can be included in the marking so as to provide useful feedback to students on those questions which they answered incorrectly (**see 25 Computer Feedback To Students**).

c Limitations can be set on the amount of time students spend on a test and the frequency with which tests can be taken. For example the screen could go blank after 15 minutes if insufficient correct answers were input by that time, and the student would then be unable to log on again for 24 hours.

d Computer records can be kept on student performance so that the teacher can easily check on student progress and identify those who have not completed many units, or who regularly take several attempts to pass tests.

e The teacher can be introduced into the system. For example when a student passes a test, an open ended question or a problem can be printed out for her to answer and submit to the teacher. The teacher gives immediate feedback and then hands out the objectives for the next unit. This is one way of dealing with those course objectives which do not readily lend themselves to objective testing.

Assessed Computer Simulations 27

Computers are used increasingly to provide sophisticated simulations of events or phenomena beyond the normal scope of conventional study: simulations of the British economy, simulations of the ecological state of a lake, simulations of human physiological functioning, simulations of the performance of a retail outlet, etc. Such simulations are frequently used in teaching, mainly as demonstrations. Students' understanding of the systems and concepts upon which the simulations are based is then usually assessed in a conventional way: by a written exam, for example. However there are a variety of ways of designing assessment directly around the use of computer simulations.

Manchester University Medical School have produced sophisticated simulations of various aspects of human functioning for training and research purposes. They are often used in biology departments to illustrate the biochemical processes involved in, for example, respiration. One such simulation, 'MACPUFF', allows the user to 'set up' a simulated patient with a chosen set of respiratory variables, in a particular atmospheric environment, and then 'run' the patient for several minutes to see what happens to various vital indicators of health and physiological functioning. Biochemical measures are calculated, listed every three seconds and plotted on graphs, and it is possible to observe the complex patterns of chemical interactions involved in maintaining a stable and healthy respiratory state.

Students' understanding of these interactions can be assessed if, for example, instructions are given to set the 'patient' up in a particular way, and then to manipulate variables (such as the amount of oxygen in the air supply) in order to stabilise the patient's condition. A full record of all interventions, and the exact consequences of these, is made automatically. A criterion referenced assessment (**see 47**) could include the requirement to stabilise the patient's condition within certain parameters, and within a time limit (perhaps 6 minutes). Such a goal cannot be achieved by trial and error, but only through an understanding of the biochemistry of respiration. The student might take many hours reading, devising intervention strategies, and then trying these out on the simulation. At the end the student would simply hand in the print-out recording the successful stabilisation of the patient, or keep a full print-out including all the unsuccessful interventions for discussion in an assessed tutorial or viva.

Computer simulations of the economy are commonplace in economics teaching. They are normally used as an illustration or perhaps as a game. But they can also be used in the same way as in the MACPUFF example above. A desired economic state for five years' hence can be specified and today's economic indicators input at the start. Students can then be set the task of achieving this desired state by manipulating those economic variables within the control of, say, the Chancellor of the Exchequer. Students can also be required to provide a commentary on the computer print-out of their economic performance, so as to demonstrate their understanding of the logic of the interaction of the variables they have manipulated.

The teaching of accountancy and financial management on computers often involves sample data in accounts software packages, and can include other elements of simulation such as company names and records of past dealings. Such material can be used as the basis of assessment tasks. For example :

Q. "Mr. Jones of TOLTREK Ltd. has an appointment with you in one hour to discuss dealings with your firm since 1 April 1984. From the database you have, prepare and print out the financial information you would require at this meeting."

Such a task has the added advantage of being similar to the real world t[illegible] student is being trained to undertake.

Computer Marked Practicals 28

Practicals in science and technology often have as their main aims:

a to get students to take accurate measurements and obtain accurate results

b to get students to make correct calculations using the correct mathematical procedures.

This causes problems for the marker. It is often not possible to tell how accurate an individual students' results are, given the errors that arise from the laboratory equipment, conditions, samples etc. Only gross inaccuracies tend to be noticed and reflected in marks, and there is no real incentive for the student to be very careful and accurate in her laboratory methods. Also, to check every student's calculations by hand can be very tedious and time consuming, and again it is common for only gross errors or the use of incorrect formulae to be spotted and reflected in marks. Finally, by the time students get their marked lab reports back it is too late to do anything about rectifying mistakes or inaccuracies, even if the students still cared about the practical. The effort students put into writing up their lab reports and the time lecturers spend marking them does not seem to lead to improvements in accuracy and technique in quantitative lab work.

These problems can be solved by the use of a computer to check on students' accuracy and calculations and to give immediate feedback to students during the lab session. To illustrate how this can be done an example of a chemistry-based computer asessment program is described.

On completing the lab work each student goes to a micro on which the appropriate programme is already running. She enters her name. The programme then asks a series of questions, eg:

Q. WHAT MASS OF SODIUM OXALATE DID YOU USE? (in grams)

The student enters all the relevant data in response to these questions. Then questions are posed which require calculations and quantitative conclusions from the data, eg:

Q. WHAT IS THE CONCENTRATION OF THE SODIUM TETRABORATE IN SOLUTION? (in moles/litre)

The programme calculates what the correct answers to these questions should be from the student's own data, and compares its own answers to those of the student, displaying feedback such as :

> Your answer to question 1
> WHAT IS THE CONCENTRATION OF THE SODIUM TETRABORATE IN SOLUTION?
> was WRONG
> you have had 1 attempt

The programme awards marks for correct answers (and fewer marks if students take several attempts) and keeps track of total marks. When the purpose of the experiment is to establish a standard value, marks are awarded to students according to how close to the class mean results they get. An individual's result which was the same as the class mean would get full marks, and results different from the mean would get proportionately fewer marks according to how many standard deviations away from the mean their results were (with a result over 4 standard deviations away getting zero).

The list of class results with their mean and standard deviation, and the individual's consequent mark, can be printed out and displayed as soon as all students have entered their data onto the micro, before the end of the lab session. In this way students get immediate feedback on their performance. This has a marked effect on the care students take in their laboratory techniques and on the overall accuracy of their results. They do their calculations during the session instead of afterwards, and as well as getting immediate feedback, have the opportunity of correcting their mistakes. A great deal of time is saved as well: the student doesn't have to write up a lab report, and the teacher doesn't have to mark it.

Although each Chemistry experiment requires a unique program which specifies the correct values and undertakes the correct calculations, the unique elements of the programme are small and simple to write. The common elements and the basic framework for eliciting students' data and allocating and recording their marks represent the major part of the programme and can easily be adapted to a variety of different quantitative experiments in any subject area in only about 15 minutes.

The programme for the chemistry practicals described here can be obtained from:

Dr. Peter Grebenik
Department of Geology and Physical Sciences
Oxford Polytechnic
Oxford OX3 0BP
U.K.

Assessing Practical and Project Work

29 Viva

30 Crits

31 Observation

32 Shared Group Grade

33 Peer Assessment of Contribution to Group

34 Second Marker's Sheet

35 Exhibition

36 Diaries and Log Books

37 Project Exam

38 The Instant Lab Report

39 Laboratory Notes

Viva 29

A viva is simply an oral exam. The most common uses of vivas are:

a the assessment of oral fluency and comprehension eg. in language learning;

b the assessment of personal qualities and attitudes;

c the assessment of the ability to think quickly and diagnose problems in novel situations eg. as a part of medical training;

d the further assessment of work previously submitted (eg. a dissertation, a design, a recording of a musical performance) in order to check that the candidate is the author of the submitted work, to explore particular questions in more depth and to explore understanding further by raising new questions.

A viva is also sometimes used where examinees lack writing skills, where written responses would be inappropriate (eg. assessing interpersonal skills), where a written test cannot easily be set (eg. for a student who missed final exams through illness), and where further information is required because written assessments have not provided unambiguous information (eg. for students with 'borderline' marks between two degree classifications).

The flexibility of vivas is their great asset. Issues can be picked up and explored in ways which are seldom possible in written tests with fixed questions which are the same for all students, and in which there is no opportunity to ask supplementary questions in cases of doubt. In even a short viva it is possible to gain a rich impression of the examinee. Examinees who do poorly in written tests but who have good oral skills may also display their knowledge better in vivas.

Problems for examiners when using vivas include:

a balancing the desire to keep the examinee relaxed with the need to ask challenging questions;

b balancing the desire to keep the examinee talking with the need to direct the examinee to areas the examiner selects;

c separating the content of what the examinee has to say from the way in which it is presented;

d turning an overall and fleeting impression gained from a small sample of behaviour into a mark or a clear assessment decision. (Few vivas, except for PhD's, take very long because they are so expensive in terms of staff time.) The vividness of an examiner's impression of a candidate may not be a sound basis for judgement;

e justifying a mark or decision afterwards in the absence of documentary evidence. Defence of viva decisions in the face of appeals tends to be based on the status and reputation of the examiner rather than on evidence.

There are also potential problems for examinees:

a it requires skills which, unlike those required for written exams, may not have been practised and developed;

b questions are likely to be less predictable than written exam questions, which makes preparation more difficult;

c it can be a very stressful experience.

Because of the potential problems vivas are often used in conjunction with other assessment methods, for the purpose of increasing the range of information available about an examinee, rather than as a replacement for other assessment methods. Some examples are:

a a brief viva with a student after reading the student's essay, but before allocating a mark to it;

b a brief viva about problems experienced during practical or project work, which are not mentioned in a written report, before allocating a mark to the report;

c a viva as a preparation for other forms of assessment: to dentify and diagnose weaknesses which require further attention from the student;

d a viva during laboratory work, to assess students' understanding of what they are doing and encourage them to be thoughtful rather than simply to follow instructions.

Crits 30

The crit is a common feature of architecture courses. After completing a major design project a student will present her design 'in public' to a group of fellow students and staff. For a small project this may be a group of half a dozen students and one or two teachers. For a major final year project it could be the entire year of students and all their teachers. A major crit might last half a day and count significantly towards the student's final qualification. In a crit the student makes a presentation explaining her design, pointing out particular aspects of the drawings: costings, construction, materials and so on, and generally selling the concepts to the audience. This is really a simulation of the architect-client relationship and relies on visual presentation and oral skills rather more than on written ability. Anyone present can ask questions eg. "Why did you do that?" "Did you reject other ideas for solving that problem?" Teachers often make suggestions eg. "Could you have solved that by.....?" "What prevented you from.......?". In a traditional crit the supervising teacher awards a mark at the end and hands the student the notes he has made during the crit as feedback.

The general model provided by the crit has several potentially valuable features which other subject areas might usefully exploit. Major projects in the social sciences could be presented in a similar way; indeed, assessed student-led seminars are a small-scale version of crits. The lack of a strong visual element would change the nature of such a crit, but there is plenty of scope for social scientists (and technologists) becoming more aware of the effectiveness of good visual presentation.

In some countries (eg. Sweden) Ph.D. theses are presented to large public gatherings and the candidate questioned by the audience rather than facing a viva (**see 29 Viva**).

The features of crits which seem worth retaining are:

a the emphasis on presentation to a live audience;

b the interactive nature of the event, with the candidate having to answer questions about purposes, compromises, omissions, justifications, etc;

c the formative assessment element, especially when new ideas and developments are suggested by the audience;

d the sense of importance and value given to students' efforts by such a major event.

Some problems can arise with the use of crits:

a students can become very nervous about presenting and defending their cherished ideas in front of an audience. Sometimes crits are experienced as gruelling events. Students may never have given such a presentation before, and the considerable weight given to the assessment increases the pressure. Six months of project work can be spoilt through stage fright;

b audience reaction can be very variable, from bland and unhelpful to downright vicious. All sorts of extraneous factors can influence this: the style and skill of the supervising teacher in chairing the crit, the time of day (crits tend to be gentle after lunch!), the degree of controversy in the presentation, and so on. The overall atmosphere cannot but influence the final mark;

c the openness of a crit can make the assessment criteria very unpredictable: these may be aesthetic criteria, technical, financial, or pragmatic criteria, environmental issues and so on. The candidate may stress historical and environmental issues in her design while the audience may place emphasis on the technical quality of the drawings or the model being used. This isn't very fair.

It is therefore important to provide clear guidelines for each of these aspects of the crit :

a train students how to give presentations, and provide clear guidelines. Give practice in the context of smaller, less important crits at an earlier stage in the course;

b provide the audience with clear guidelines about how to be a helpful, fair audience. Agree a procedure for the structure and conduct of the crit which prevents it getting out of hand. Provide guidelines for the supervising teacher about how to chair crits;

c either:

- specify criteria to be used for assessing all crits, reminding students of them at the outset of their projects and reminding the audience at the start of the crit (**see 41 Project Criteria**);

or

- establish specific criteria for each project (**see 46 Negotiating Criteria**) and inform the audience of them at the start of each crit.

They will then be able to judge the presentation according to appropriate criteria.

Observation 31

Observation is a common method of assessment in some subjects. For example, teacher training involves extended periods of classroom practice which are assessed by observation of the way the student handles the class. In Britain it is not possible to qualify as a teacher without passing this element of the assessment. Laboratory work too is often observed for assessment purposes (though not as often as might be sensible: laboratory reports hide as much as they reveal!) Practical training, from hairdressing to motor vehicle maintenance, generally involves observing and assessing the student in action. In these cases the use of observation is an explicit, formal part of the assessment system.

In many situations, however, observation goes on a good deal but only informally affects assessment. For example in studio-based work (eg. art, design, architecture) the teacher will spend a lot of time observing the students working, but the assessment is, ostensibly, only of the end product: drawings, designs, plans or whatever. The final assessments are bound to be strongly influenced by the observations the teacher has made of the way these products were arrived at. It might be fairer in such circumstances to be explicit about the role of observation and about the criteria actually being used (for example, speed of working, ability to learn from mistakes, use of equipment, etc.) These criteria could be listed for students to see, to make them aware of what the observation consists of and orient them towards better practice (**see 40 Criteria for Students**).

In many areas where process is at least as important as product there is scope for using observation in a formal way by, for example:

a observing and marking laboratory practice instead of marking lab reports;

b observing and marking students' seminar performance instead of marking their seminar papers;

c observing students on field work (eg. geology or surveying) instead of marking their reports and maps.

The main objection to using observation in assessment is that it is subjective and open to personal bias. Without a concrete product such as a report a student cannot appeal to a second marker (though student teachers can appeal to an external examiner who then observes them teaching another class). To reduce this problem you can:

a use observation checklists so that marks are related to specific behaviours rather than a global judgement;

b use clear criteria with marks awarded for each criterion;

c use records such as audio tapes or video tapes which can be examined afterwards by a third party if neccessary. (They can also be used to give extra feedback to the student.)

Assessing group project work

In group project work, students work as teams in small groups. Each group does a project and produces a report. One mark is then awarded to each group.

This type of assessment can give rise to problems, between groups and within groups.

Problems between groups relate to the level and range of marks. First, group work tends to be marked higher than individual work: groups can achieve more than individuals, and individual weaknesses tend to be covered up by other group members' strengths. Second, group marks tend to vary less than individual marks. If groups are randomly formed, the average ability of the members of the groups will be similar and will lead to a narrow overall spread of marks. On many courses it is unacceptable for marks to be uniformly high (or, to put it technically, for the mean to be high and the standard deviation small).

Problems within groups relate to the differential contributions made by the group members. It is common for some students to contribute more than others to the production of the group report. Those who contribute less (either quantitatively or qualitatively) may deserve a lower mark than those who contribute more. Normally, however, group members are given the same grade because differences between group members' contributions are not apparent to the marker, who only sees the final report and not the process by which it came to be written. In this situation it is possible for low contributors to be 'carried' by the high contributors without incurring a penalty. The difficulty of arriving at a fair mark for individuals is one of the most common reasons for not using group work for assessment purposes, despite its many advantages for learning.

Some courses cope with these problems by reducing the overall contribution of group marks to the course mark, so that the problems don't have too great an effect. A more satisfactory solution is to try to build in mechanisms to allocate different marks to the different members of a group which reflect their relative contributions to the group's work.

The first method described (**see 32 Shared Group Grade**) is fairer to individuals, and increases the spread of marks.

The second method (**see 33 Peer Assessment of Contribution to Group**) achieves both these aims and in addition lowers the average mark.

Shared Group Grade 32

While the teacher may not have much idea about individual students' contributions to a group project, the students themselves are in a very good position to make such judgements. Though the teacher can only award a mark to the group, the members of that group can be left to distribute the mark between themselves in a way which they think reflects the relative contributions of individuals. For example if a group of five students were to be awarded 60% for a group report, they would be given 5 x 60 = 300 marks to distribute amongst themselves.

There are three ways in which groups tend to react in this situation:

a some groups will agree at the start of the project that all marks will be shared equally at the end, in order to avoid unpleasantness. Such groups must face the prospect of individual group members doing little work, safe in the knowledge that they will get the same mark as the rest of the group;

b other groups will not discuss assessment at all until it comes to dividing up the marks. They then find that they disagree about the basis upon which the marks should be divided. Some will value creativity, some will value workload, some will value leadership, some will value the ability to communicate the project outcomes, and so on. Without prior agreement about criteria there are likely to be arguments about who should get what marks for which contributions;

c some groups will sit down at the start and decide what criteria they will use in allocating marks, and will keep to these criteria. Everyone will be clear about what their contribution ought to be, and will be more likely to accept the final allocation of marks.

This third way of dealing with shared group grades is clearly the most satisfactory and you can help your students by organising discussion and negotiation of criteria at the start of the project. If you don't have time for this, you can impose criteria of your own which the students then use to allocate the marks. It is crucial, however, that the criteria are made clear and accepted at the start of the project, and not pulled out of thin air at the end.

There are two rather different ways in which criteria can be used:

a students may naturally adopt different working roles within the group, or the project may even specify such roles. For example one student may become the chairperson, one the note-taker, one the data-analyser, one the report writer, one the 'ideas person' and so on. In this case assessment criteria can focus on how well each student performed her different role;

b every student may be expected to contribute equally to all aspects of the project (for example each writing one section of a group report). In this case each criterion should be applied equally to each student. In **33 Peer Assessment of Contribution to Group** there is a list of criteria which could be used in this way.

Peer Assessment of Contribution to Group

33

One solution to the problems associated with assessment of group project work - of unfairness to individuals, high average marks, and narrow bands of marks - is to weight an individual's marks according to her contribution to the group's work. Contributions are best judged by the group itself. In the rating sheet given as an example on page 108, group members are required to rate every other member of the group in terms of several key aspects of their contribution to the group's work. The criteria used here are for illustration only: other criteria concerning creativity, supportiveness in the group, or ability to keep to deadlines could equally be used. The average rating for each individual is then deducted from the group mark and allocated to that individual as her mark. In this case a student who made a major contribution to the group's work in every respect would have an average rating of 0 and receive the group grade. A student who contributed little to the group's work in all of these respects would receive the group grade minus 20 marks.

More or less severe penalties could be devised either by varying the number of criteria used, or by varying the penalties associated with criteria. The relative importance of criteria can be reflected in different penalties, as in the example overleaf. The criteria and size of penalties can be negotiated with the students, or even determined by them, at the start of the project so that they are aware of how they will be assessed, and have a commitment to the criteria.

PEER ASSESSMENT OF CONTRIBUTION TO GROUP - RATING SHEET

Student... has contributed to the group's work in the following ways:

	Major Contribution	Some Contribution	Little Contribution
1. Leadership and direction	0	-1	-2
2. Organisation and management	0	-1	-2
3. Ideas and suggestions	0	-1	-2
4. Data collection	0	-2	-4
5. Data analysis	0	-2	-4
6. Report writing	0	-3	-6
Total penalty			

Second Marker's Sheet 34

It is common for certain pieces of students' work to be assessed by two people rather than one in order to increase reliability and fairness. The larger and more important the piece of work (for example a final year project in a degree course) the more likely it is that a second marker will be involved.

Disagreements between markers arise for many reasons, some of which it is impossible to do anything about. But there is one important difference between the first and second marker which frequently leads to dissent and which can easily be remedied. The first marker is almost invariably the student's teacher or supervisor and will know the student and be aware of how she has tackled the project. The second marker is unlikely to know anything about this and will have to award marks without any contextual information. Some of this information is crucial to a fair assessment of the project. For example did the student receive a great deal of help in carying out the work? Was the original idea for the work the student's own? Was a first draft submitted to and improved by the student's teacher or supervisor? While it is possible to mark a piece of work 'on its own merits' without regard for such information, assessment criteria usually include such factors as the initiative taken by the student, the creativity of the student and so on. Such criteria can only be implemented with the knowledge of the context in which the work was undertaken.

To give an example of the problems which can arise, a student could have left it until the last minute to start a project, then sought the advice of her supervisor for a suitable topic, been given help with references and experimental design, been given help with analysis and interpretation and been given detailed comments on a first draft of the report. The student might then submit quite a good final report.

The first marker would know that little of this was the student's own work and give a moderate mark whilst a second marker would simply mark the report as seen and award a high mark.

To get around such problems you can simply provide the second marker with information about the way the work was carried out. One way of doing this is shown in the Second Marker's Sheet on page 111. The information in this checklist is in the form of rating scales so as to provide information quickly and in a form which is easy to interpret. The supervisor completes this form and hands it to the second marker along with the student's work.

SECOND MARKER'S SHEET

Name of Student ....

Supervisor ....

Second Marker ....

	suggested to student		received normal assistance		entirely student's own
1. Choice of topic	1	2	3	4	5
2. Theoretical contribution	1	2	3	4	5
3. Contribution to experimental design	1	2	3	4	5
4. Experimental technique	1	2	3	4	5
5. Data analysis and statistical treatment of results	1	2	3	4	5
6. Interpretation of results	1	2	3	4	5
	poor		normal		good
7. Impression of student's grasp of topic	1	2	3	4	5
	light		normal		heavy
8. Workload involved in the topic	1	2	3	4	5

Additional remarks from supervisor

....

....

Suggested Mark.................................. Signed..

Exhibition 35

It is usual for students on visual arts courses to exhibit their work, either as individual items or in collections which give a fuller impression of its range and quality. The exhibition can be used for assessment in a variety of other areas too. It can accompany oral presentation (**see 30 Crits**) or stand alone and be judged as an independent item.

For example on one geography course students are required to produce a poster portraying one of the concepts of the course in a striking and informative way. The posters are exhibited for all to see and assessed without the support of verbal justifications by students.

Scientific and project work can also be exhibited, with photographs of equipment, clear graphs and diagrams, summaries and layouts to portray work undertaken. This encourages an emphasis on communication skills, especially graphic skills and the ability to write brief and clear summaries. It also tends to highlight the need to identify and and demonstrate the purpose and conclusions of the project. Exhibitions 'sell' ideas and are used extensively in industry; this is a form of communication which students can benefit from encountering at first hand.

The preparation of exhibitions can be very engaging for students, and viewing them can be of great interest to others. So much of student learning is undertaken privately, even secretively, that an exhibition can have a powerful impact on students' motivation.

Exhibitions also lend themselves to student participation in assessment. The viewing of an exhibition is in itself evaluatory and students can view and assess each other's work in exhibitions faster and more conveniently than through most other techniques. If students are to mark each other's exhibitions then it can help to have an agreed set of criteria (see **40 Criteria for Students**). Otherwise, in the absence of agreed criteria, there is a danger that viewers will be influenced by impressive graphics at the expense of other aspects of the exhibition.

Diaries and Log Books 36

A diary or log book is an individual record in which a student charts, day by day or week by week, her experience of a course or part of a course. It can be set as an alternative to or in addition to more traditional types of assessed writing.

The diary is different from the essay or report in that it focusses on the process of learning rather than the outcome and also in that it tends to be informal in style and structure.

The diary is a particularly appropriate method of assessment where the whole point of a course is what the students experience. The experience is not available from textbooks or lectures and has to be identified by the participants themselves.

The rubric for the assessed diary could be, for example:

> "Keep a diary in which you write a brief summary of the activities of each week's session. Say what you have learned about yourself and others."

Or it could be less structured:

> "Keep a diary in which you write anything you like about your thoughts and feelings on the course."

It may be helpful, especially when students have not been assessed in this way before, if they are encouraged to read each other's diaries after a few weeks, so that they can see the potential of the diary form. Or they could read an extract from a published diary: for example the autobiography of Eamon Dunphy, the Millwall footballer of the 60's, illustrates what a reflective diary can look like.

Another variation is that each week just one member of the class writes the diary episode, copies of which are then distributed to the rest of the students, so that they finish with a group record of the course. This can encourage group cohesiveness and trust, and it cuts down on the work for each individual. These diary episodes can be assessed and contribute to course marks.

The diary can also be used in conjunction with more formal types of assessed written work such as, for example, write-ups of science practicals, reports on industrial placements and work experience, and project reports of all kinds. If students have kept a record of experience as it happened, they have the opportunity afterwards to reflect upon the progress they have made and the directions they have chosen.

The rubric for a science practical could be:

> "As you do this set of experiments, keep a log of everything you do and everything you observe, even if you can't see its relevance."

The rubric for students on sandwich placements could be:

> "At the end of each day, briefly note down your impressions and your thoughts. Even if your experience seems disjointed at first, it will make more sense later if you have notes to look back on."

And for other kinds of project:

> "Keep a diary of all the work you do for this project : books and articles read, action taken, decisions made, and also dead ends, apparently wasted effort, etc. Your diary should also contain a section specifying what you have learned from doing this project."

Students involved in design projects, in such subjects as architecture, are often required to keep copies of all early drawings, including even rejected scribblings, together with rough notes on them. This kind of 'working diary' can help the teacher to assess the finished product with a better understanding of how it was achieved, and also to give feedback to the student on crucial design decisions, short cuts and so on.

The diary can also be used as a way into other more conventional academic forms of writing. The student who says she has a 'block' about writing essays or reports can be encouraged to sort out her ideas first in a diary where she is not under pressure to conform to a particular structure or style. Then, when she has got her ideas on paper, she should have the confidence to re-write them as an essay or report.

Criteria for assessing diaries can be similar to those for other written work. Though there are no strict rules about structure or writing style, students can still be judged on such criteria as originality, commitment, skills of analysis and synthesis, sensitivity, self knowledge etc. It is important to be explicit to students about criteria (**see 41 Project Criteria**) or to devise criteria together with students so that they understand then and are committed to them (**see 42 Negotiating Criteria**).

The Project Exam 37

There are occasions where the main learning activity on a course is some kind of practical or project work but where there is still some necessity for a formal written examination. This may be because external validating bodies or professional bodies require an exam. Or it may be because the teachers consider an exam to be desirable.

Conventional exams, with their tendency to emphasise memorising and regurgitation of factual information, are quite unsuitable for a project-based course. They can completely distort the aims of the course by distracting students from their project work because they know that they are not going to be tested on it in the exam. However there are forms of exam which avoid these problems by asking students questions directly related to their project work.

On one estate management course students undertook a substantial case study involving the simulated purchase of a building site and its subsequent commercial development. This they wrote up in a report consisting of a log of their calculations, decisions, problems, etc. (**see 42 Log Book**). The examination questions could take the form:

Q. If there was a three month national building strike starting on week 3 of the simulation, how would this affect your handling of the case?

Q. If outline planning consent were granted for a competing major shopping precinct at the north end of the High Street on week 14 of the simulation (see details below), how would you advise your client?

Students would have their log books and other case material to hand (**see 20 Open Book Exam**) and would be expected to use these in answering the questions. Such questions cannot be answered from memory, or even directly from this information, but only from students' experience and understanding of the case study.

In this first example, all students undertook the same project work individually. In the second example, below, students had been working in separate groups and individuals had been awarded a group grade (but see **32 Shared Group Grade** and **33 Peer Assessment of Contribution to Group**). The exam in this case was designed to test individuals' understanding and to produce a mark for each individual student. The context was a catering management course in which groups of about 8 students tackled a simulated management problem. Within the groups students performed different roles (for example secretary, report writer) and so they almost certainly learned different things. The course was designed to apply management principles to a specific and complex situation. An exam was used to test individuals' ability to apply these principles to the work of their own groups.

Exam questions could take the form:

Q. How can pricing and marketing policies influence other management decisions concerning catering outlets? Give specific examples from the simulation to illustrate your points.

The first part of this question is general, in that it is based on management principles learned at an earlier stage in the course. It is the second part which tests students' ability to apply these principles to their project work. This type of exam has the added advantage that if students know at the outset that they will be expected to answer questions of this form, they are more likely to be reflective about theory and general principles during the simulation than to get overwhelmed with practical details and forget the purpose of the exercise.

be expected to answer [illegible], they are more likely to be reflective about theory and general principles [illegible] to overwhelmed with practical detail and [illegible] purpose of the exercise.

The Instant Lab Report 38

Experienced scientists make full notes of their procedure, observations and results in the laboratory as they go along. Preliminary calculations are often made immediately in order to check that nothing is going seriously wrong. In contrast students are usually expected to produce neat lab reports for assessment at a later date, sometimes much later. The effect this often has is to focus students' attention on producing good finished products, and to encourage leisurely post-hoc analysis and description of what happened, if not actual fiddling of results. Marks reflect students' abilities outside the lab rather than in it. Another effect is that students tend to work less quickly during practicals, noticing less about what is going on, and reflecting less about this. They follow instructions and adopt a narrow technical approach rather than a wider scientific approach to experimental work.

If instead lab reports are required to be handed in at the end of the practical, this can have a dramatic effect on the way students undertake their work. They are likely to work faster, try to make more sense of what they are doing, make more observations and record these in better organised notes, and take more care when recording data. Obvious errors are more likely to be picked up, especially if calculations are undertaken immediately, and there may even be the opportunity to do the work again and get it right.

There is a risk that the quality of presentation may suffer if reports are written in the lab. Teachers can respond by:

a accepting that reports will not look so good, and simply changing the criteria used in allocating marks, with full recording of procedures and results carrying more weight than neatness;

b giving students uncompleted handouts on which they record procedures and results under headings and fill in spaces in response to questions. The amount of material on the handout can be reduced over time as students become more competent at writing their own reports as they go along. Initially it may be necessary to produce a handout specific to the experiment being undertaken, with standard details (eg. materials and methods) typed in, and only a small number of sections for the students to complete. In time this can be reduced to a standard 'all-purpose' experimental report form containing only headings.

Apart from clear benefits to student learning during practicals, this method frees students afterwards to do something more constructive than trying to remember what happened last week in order to write up a neat report. It also saves the teacher's time, as 'instant' lab reports tend to be much shorter than those written afterwards.

Laboratory Notes 39

Experienced scientists keep a notebook at hand during experimental work. They write down exactly what they do, what they notice, what goes wrong, what thoughts they have and so on. Notes are vital to the process of interpreting results and writing up an adequate account of the experiment. Some notes are so thorough that it is a only a short step from them to a full report.

Inexperienced students, in contrast, tend to take few and scrappy notes. Without material provided by the lecturer they would find it impossible to remember the experiment and to write a full account of it. Much 'fudging' of evidence and interpretation goes on afterwards because students simply do not have full notes from which to construct a full and honest report. This lack of notetaking may result from poor observation, or may even cause it: if no use is made of observations then there is little point in making them. Students can end up doing experiments by simply following instructions in a mindless way.

If you want to encourage a more scientific and active approach to experimental work, and more observation and reflection during practicals, you can assess students' laboratory notebooks. This can be done as well as, or instead of, assessing laboratory reports which are written up afterwards.

Students may need guidance in taking laboratory notes. You could:

a recommend a particular type of notebook;

b suggest headings and specific items;

c show examples of useful lab notes;

d have an exhibition of all students' notebooks half way through the year to guide future notetaking (**see 35 Exhibition**);

e pass students' notebooks round the class for comment and comparison;

f clarify your criteria for assessing such notes. eg.

fullness
range of observations
clarity
neatness
adequacy of diagrams
specification of units
etc.

(**see also 40 Criteria for Students**)

It is important, in assessing notebooks, that you do not pervert their purpose. If students start handing in second drafts, neat versions, and notes which were obviously written largely after the experimental work, in order to get better marks, then you may have to take other action to retrieve the situation (eg. **see 38 Instant Lab Report**).

Lab notebooks may also be used to record subsequent thoughts derived from further reading, analysis of data, seminars and so on. The notebook then becomes a record of the development of students' understanding of the subject, and can be used as the basis for reflection. You could suggest that two pages headed 'thoughts' or 'discussion' be left blank between experiments, to be completed at a later stage as ideas arise.

It is common for such lab notebooks to be handed in only at the end of the year. However the process of writing such a notebook can encourage so much reflection, self assessment and learning that it can be valuable to make them more central to the learning process by:

a assessing them regularly eg. every four weeks;

b organising seminars, tutorials or more informal discussions around them;

c encouraging students to share and discuss their notes in small groups, without a teacher present, during the last 10 minutes of a practical class.

Criteria

Criteria for Students 40

One of the most effective ways of getting students to write assignments in the way you want them to, and to improve the quality of their assignments, is simply to tell them what your assessment criteria are. If students know how marks are gained and lost this will have a powerful effect on their behaviour.

Sometimes these criteria are hidden, or at least may seem so to students (**see 46**). Even when guidelines for writing assignments are provided, students do not always recognise that they also contain implicit, or even explicit, marking criteria. For example one set of guidelines, "Notes on the presentation of experimental reports" for psychology students, contains predictable sections on layout, headings and so on, but also advice such as:

> "Individual style and opinion are of little interest compared with a clear and lucid description....Personal opinions should be avoided as far as possible and where mentioned should be identified as such....Use of the first person singular should be avoided".

Criteria such as these are not only related to marking; they define the whole nature of the learning task which students are confronted with. It is vital that students recognise them if they are to go about their studying in an appropriate way.

Sometimes criteria are specific to a particular subject, or to the way that subject happens to be taught in a particular institution - and are quite unpredictable to an outsider. For example, one set of "Guidelines on essay writing" for geography students illustrates such local criteria:

"(ii) subheadings are necessary. These should not necessarily be one-word telepathic subheads - they should express concisely what is to be found in the section following them. (Do not get the wrong idea about subheads - they do not 'break up' an essay - on the contrary, they make it flow and integrate the elements of argument in the reader's mind. They make for vastly greater clarity - most published academic work uses them, so do most newspapers - in both communication is important. USE SUBHEADS!)"

In a different department just along the corridor from these geographers, students are marked down when they use subheadings, let alone the kind of grammar and punctuation used here. So it is clearly important to let the students know exactly what the local criteria are.

The criteria in the two examples above are general in the sense that they apply to all reports, or all essays, in a subject area. However it is often the case that criteria vary considerably from one assessed task to another, and even from one teacher to another, even within a subject area, in a way which reflects a range of different educational goals. For example scientific laboratory work can be undertaken for many different reasons:

- to develop skills with equipment
- to demonstrate phenomena
- to develop general scientific methodology
- to aid the grasp of new concepts
- to improve report writing
- to increase accuracy in measurement
- to practise mathematical methods

and so on. These different aims are likely to be reflected in marking criteria, if not in the form of reports students are required to write. It is crucial that students are told what they should be concentrating on. A briefing could take the following form:

> "The experiment today involves sensitive and tricky equipment which is new to you, and difficult measurements. Even small errors in your measurements will invalidate the experiment. So you should concentrate on accuracy, and on calculating the degree of error involved in your measurements and calculations. I'm not interested, today, in a long theoretical introduction to your reports, or an extended discussion of your results. Concentrate on measurement issues and error. You will be marked largely on how accurate your results are".

Such concerns can be operationalised by allocating marks to explicit criteria. For example the standard form on page 134 requires the teacher to fill in the 'guidelines' and 'maximum marks' before the lab work is undertaken. Handing this form out to students makes it clear how marks will be awarded for this particular piece of work. The form is returned by the student with the completed report, and the teacher uses it both to allocate marks and to give feedback to students by writing comments under the different headings.

Explicit criteria like this are not just educationally effective in that they succeed in alerting students to the requirements for a satisfactory piece of work. They are also fairer in that they counteract 'halo' effects in marking whereby presentation, for example, has a disproportionate effect on marks and a neatly typed report is preferred to a scruffy one regardless of content. Explicit criteria also increase the likelihood that different markers will come up with the same marks.

LABORATORY REPORT MARKING SHEET

COURSE...

EXPERIMENT TITLE..

REPORT SECTIONS	GUIDELINES	MAX MARK	YOUR MARK	COMMENTS
INTRODUCTION				
METHOD				
RESULTS				
DISCUSSION				
CONCLUSION				
GENERAL CRITERIA				
ACCURACY				
PRESENTATION				
	TOTAL	100		

OVERALL COMMENTS :

....

....

....

Project Criteria 41

The arguments for having clear assessment criteria for project work are much the same as those for having criteria for any other kind of work (**see 40 Criteria for Students**) but projects pose additional problems. In essay writing it is th product which is assessed and, while the skills and processes by which the product was produced may be assessed indirectly, these are not open to scrutiny. In project work the process is often the most important element, and the skills involved in undertaking the project and presenting its outcomes are usually far more important than the outcomes themselves. Since the choice of criteria dictates the direction and form of project work, criteria for marking projects should clearly reflect these different educational goals and direct students' attention towards these goals.

A second difficulty with project criteria is that projects tend to be open-ended: outcomes are inherently unpredictable. This means that criteria need to be couched in somewhat general terms. Criteria which specify content on the one hand or criteria which specify form or process on the other hand will tend to result in a narrowing of the scope of the project. For short projects, for inexperienced students, and when educational goals for the project are tightly specified in terms of content, this may be desirable. For open-ended projects designed to give students scope for exploration and creativity such criteria would be counterproductive.

The concern for process and for open-endedness is illustrated in the following extract from a list of criteria used by more than 50 mathematics lecturers at the University of Southampton:

"Supervisors are reminded that their assessment of the way in which the student has worked during the course is to be taken into account together with the assessment of the dissertation. This should be reflected in the written comments, and may be relevant to the criteria under headings B and C below.

A Exposition	Mathematical accuracy
	Clarity
	Literary presentation
B Literature	Understanding
	Relating different sources
	Finding new sources
C Originality	Examples cited
	Examples constructed
	New treatments and proofs of standard results
	Simple generalisations
	Original researches
D Scope of topic	Conceptual difficulty
	Technical difficulty
	Relationship with previous studies
	Relevance of material included
	Coverage of the topic"

The example on page 138 includes not just a detailed set of criteria, but a grading scheme for each criterion, and a system of allocating marks under each of the main headings. It can serve as a profile at the same time as being used as a marking scheme (**see 45 Profiles and 43 Marking Schemes**). It contains an element of flexiblity in that some criteria can be ruled inapplicable and other new criteria can be added. Many of the criteria here are concerned exclusively with process and skills and could not be applied in a situation where assessment is based on the final report alone. For example, in section 1.6 the student's log book is assessed (**see also 36 Diaries and Log Books**). These criteria, focussing as they do on process, entail close supervision by the teacher throughout the project.

These criteria also reflect a further interesting characteristic of projects: the extended period of time usually associated with project work allows proper revision and redrafting of final reports. Here the draft report is allocated more marks than the final report, and criteria for the final report include the response of the student to criticism of the draft. Criteria for the draft are concerned with substantive issues, while those for the final report are concerned with presentation and style. The example is taken from the School of Engineering at the University of Bath.

PROJECT MARKING FORM

MARKS ALLOCATION

Carrying out	(50%)	%
Log Book	(5%)	%
Draft Report	(30%)	%
Final Report	(15%)	%
		%

Supervisors should enter their grading of the student's performance under these headings: they should indicate where they are inapplicable, and add any special aspects in section 4. The items are not weighted, so there is no requirement to convert the gradings into marks.

O=outstanding E=excellent G=good S=satisfactory P=poor I=inadequate

	O	E	G	S	P	I	COMMENTS
1. <u>CARRYING OUT</u>							
1.1 Approach							
Exploration and enquiry							
Literature and background search							
Setting objectives							
Preparation of programme							
1.2 Implementation							
Decisions on test facilities and instrumentation							

O=outstanding E=excellent G=good S=satisfactory P=poor I=inadequate							
	O	E	G	S	P	I	COMMENTS
Design of rigs and apparatus Building and commissioning rigs Setting up calibration							
1.3 Experiments Logical planning Accuracy and relevance of measurements Overcoming difficulties Modifications during progress							
1.4 Computing Modelling Programming Analysis Presentation							
1.5 Evaluation Study of previous theories Prediction based on theory Analysis of experimental results Relation between theory and results							

		O	E	G	S	P	I	COMMENTS
1.6	Log Book Maintained as instructed Standard of entries							
2.	MANUSCRIPT DRAFT REPORT Structure of the report Clarity of argument Balance of sections Validity of results Justification of conclusions Details; figures; titles; references Achievement of objectives							
3.	FINAL REPORT Response to criticisms of draft Layout of report Standard of execution Style							
4.	SPECIAL ASPECTS							
5.	SUPERVISOR'S COMMENTS ON STUDENT'S PERFORMANCE AND ATTITUDES eg. response to advice and criticism, initiative, determination to succeed, dependence on instruction, powers of innovation, enthusiasm, perseverance							

Negotiating Criteria 42

If criteria for assessment exist in any explicit form they are normally fixed by the teacher. They may provide information for students during assessments such as exams (**see 43 Marking Schemes**) or guide the way students approach assessed tasks (**see 40 Criteria for Students**) but they are still imposed by the teacher. An alternative is for students to negotiate their own criteria. This ensures not only that they know what the criteria are, but also that they understand and endorse them. It also gives students the opportunity to make their own proposals about assessment.

There are various ways in which you can enable your students to negotiate their own criteria.

If they are used to taking responsibility for their own learning it may be enough just to say to them: "I suggest that you negotiate your own criteria for the essays you write on this course. What I'll do is allow half an hour at the end of this session for you to discuss assessment and draw up a list of criteria." You may like to stay and observe their discussion so that you understand the thinking behind their conclusions or you may feel that they will work better if you leave them to work on their own.

If your students need a structured activity you can suggest that they all note down individually the characteristics of "the best essay I ever wrote" or that they get into groups and note down the characteristics of "the perfect essay". These notes can then form the basis for the discussion of criteria.

An alternative method is to start from criteria which are already in operation. For this each student will need to have a piece of work which you have marked. They analyse the feedback and grade that you have given them and infer what criteria you used. Or students in pairs can read each other's essays and give each other feedback from which the criteria are inferred. The group then decides whether these are criteria that they are happy with or whether they can improve on them.

Whatever method your students use to arrive at their criteria, you need to ensure that they end up with a clear list which everyone understands and agrees to.

Marking Schemes 43

Marking schemes consist of information concerning how marks are allocated to answers. They perform two main functions: one for the student and one for the marker.

For the student it is possible to specify, on a question paper, how marks are to be distributed between questions. For example it is common in science subjects for the first section to contain factual and short answer questions and for the second section to contain larger and more open-ended problems requiring more understanding. Typically the questions in the first section each attract fewer marks than those in the section section, and even if there are more questions in the first section, and it takes up more space on the paper, fewer marks are allocated to the section. It is important for students to recognise this if they are to distrbute their time and effort sensibly between questions. In fact understanding the balance of such marking schemes is crucial to learning strategies during the course and to revision techniques before exams.

Marking schemes can be used even more specifically to orient students' effort in desired directions. For example with structured questions containing several elements **(see 3 Structured Essays)** it is helpful to students to specify the marks which will be allocated to each element.

Marking schemes also perform useful functions for the marker. Where many different markers are involved in assessing answers to the same questions it is common practice to use marking schemes which refer explicitly to the content of answers. A common type of marking scheme specifies particular items which should for example be mentioned by students, briefly discussed, or presented in diagrams. Students accumulate marks according to how many of these specified 'targets' they manage to hit. The purpose of such marking schemes is to increase the consistency with which different markers award marks to the same answer.

The following example illustrates the two main purposes of marking schemes. First, the exam paper:

"TEC Higher Certificate in Applied Biology Year 1 198 /8

MICROBIOLOGY THEORY

Instructions: Answer BOTH questions in Section A (40%) and any THREE in Section B (60%)

SECTION A (40%)

2. In an experiment to determine the rate.......
(a description of an experiment, and some experimental data, followed)

Answer each of the following:

(a) Plot the data on a single side of graph paper and in the most appropriate manner. (12 marks)

(b) Calculate the mean generation time of the bacterium in the two media. (2 marks)

(c) Explain why the inoculum was washed and predict the likely result of the experiment if the innoculum had been taken directly from a nutrient broth culture. (4 marks)

(d) In this experiment, colony counts were used to determine the increase in population size during the incubation. Suggest another method which could have been used to measure the increase. (2 marks)"

Without this guidance on the way marks were to be allocated it seems unlikely that students would have guessed that the calculation in section(b) and the suggestion in section (d) were only worth a sixth of the marks of the graph in section (a). This guidance should result in students spending more than half the time allocated for this question on the graph in section (a).

A teacher's marking scheme was written for this exam paper. The scheme for question 2 is reproduced below. The number of marks which can be awarded for each element of the answer is specified, as is the maximum number of marks for each section.

"ANSWERS:

2. (a) Graph (12 marks)

Title: **Growth**(0.5) of a **bacterium**(0.5) in **two media**(0.5) at **30°C** (0.5) with **aeration**(0.5).

X-axis: **time**(0.5); **hours**(0.5); **sensible scale**(0.5).

Y-axis: **counts**(0.5); **volume**(0.5); **log plot**(0.5); **sensible scale**(0.5).

Plots: **correct plot** of each set of data(2.0); **sensible line** for growth pattern for each set of data(2.0); **zero time count** calculated(2.0).

(b)(2 marks) **2 values** within 10%(2.0).

(c)(4 marks) To **remove** nutrient broth from innoculum(2.0). **No lag phase** in nutrient broth(1.0). **Growth rates** of cells in defined medium would be **different**(1.0).
Any other sensible suggestions(1.0).

(d)(4 marks) **Absorption**(2.0).
Any other reasonable suggestion(2.0).

20 marks total "

This kind of marking scheme can increase consistency between markers. It can also cause unfairness if students offer valid comments, or go about answering questions, in ways which are not mentioned in the scheme. Attempts to allow for such variation (eg. "Any sensible suggestion") somewhat undermine the purpose of the scheme. In addition it might be considered whether it would be fairer for students be told about those elements of the marking scheme which concern the balance of marks between aspects of the answer.

Staff Marking Exercise 44

If you were to ask the members of a course team what their criteria for assessment were, it is likely that the answers would be so general and all-embracing as to be unhelpful. Such generalisations can also mask real differences in teachers' values and perceptions of the aims of a course. One way of highlighting these is to run a staff marking exercise. In a staff marking exercise, teachers get together with copies of pieces of student work on the same topic, mark them, and compare their marks and comments. This then leads to a general discussion about assessment. The purpose of this is not to mark the students, but to provide a forum in which teachers can find out about how they compare with each other. In particular it can clarify the criteria that are being used in assessment.

In the Open University, where many people will be teaching on the same course, it is common at the start of the year to get all the teachers together and give them some samples of student work to mark. The ensuing discussions help to clarify the aims of the course, and also encourage consistency between markers. Teachers can see very quickly whether they are adopting different standards and marking more strictly or more generously than their colleagues.

Even when a set of criteria for student assignments exists (**see 40 Criteria for Students**) these may not lead to consistency between markers if there are valu differences. For example teachers often put a different value on the dutiful, painstaking but dull piece of work and the quirky, unstructured witty piece. It is easy to include these elements in a list of criteria, but harder to be explicit about their relative importance. Staff marking exercises give an opportunity to explore these issues.

The following points are offered as guidance for marking exercises:

a choose real examples of student work as a basis for discussion. Abstract dicussions are much less fruitful. Even one example is very much better than none. Three or four examples are usually plenty: more can cause confusion and introduce more complexity and variation than staff can handle;

b choose examples of moderate quality or perhaps of uneven quality containing both good and bad features. It is relatively easy to agree on what is outstanding or awful, and little is learned through such easy agreements;

c get staff to mark the examples all at the same time, during the exercise. If they do the marking too far in advance there is a danger that they will either have forgotten details or formed a fixed and limited impression, perhaps with the expectation of having to defend it in public;

d do not at first expect staff to make public their marks or views of the examples. Allow them the opportunity to compare these with one or two others 'in private' first. This will make it much more likely that they will be flexible and receptive to the reality of differing values and perceptions which will inevitably be revealed;

e an attempt should be made to extract and discuss broad differences of principle and values underlying the differences in marks even if this proves difficult, rather than to go straight into seeking compromise and consensus on marks. There is unlikely to be any long term effect on consistency unless the broad issues are tackled;

f outcomes of the exercise should be clearly recorded to avoid staff sliding back into their old patterns;

g students should be informed of issues which have been resolved concerning criteria and standards.

Profiles 45

The outcome of most assessment systems is a single grade or mark which is meant to indicate the student's overall ability or achievement. This grade or mark may have been arrived at through the assessment of many distinct areas of knowledge and skills, and the student is likely to have achieved more in some areas than others. None of these different achievements, or weaknesses, are reflected in the final mark in a way which can be interpreted by an outsider (or even by the student or her teacher in many cases). Profiling has the opposite goal. The aim of profiling in not to summarise all the component elements in a single mark but to represent the component elements separately. Its purpose is primarily informative: to provide the student, the teacher, and outsiders, with information which can guide further learning, teaching and selection. A final mark is almost entirely summative in nature: it simply indicates something about what has been achieved. Profiles are formative as well as summative in that in addition they highlight the areas where the need for further learning is indicated.

By specifying the key elements on which assessment is based, profiling also identifies criteria. Very often this is done through the statement of objectives ie. statements of what the student should be able to <u>do</u> at the end of the course. The final profile, or assessment summary, can be seen as a statement of which objectives have been achieved and also, perhaps, to what standard.

The example on page 153 of a profile statement is taken from a B/TEC Mathematics I Unit which is part of a course in Technician Studies. The breakdown of general objectives makes it clear what is to be learnt. The performance indicator is designed to show the extent to which the objectives have been achieved. This form can be updated as the student is assessed. A full profile of the student's learning is available at each stage in the course, indicating where further effort is called for, and where assessment is required. At the end of the course the profile indicates what the student can do, and can not do, and any gaps will indicate areas where the student's ability has not been established.

The use of profiles has become widespread in the assessment of personal qualities, partly out of a desire to provide clear criteria and reduce variability between different assessors, but also to provide feedback for students and information for future employers. As with all uses of criteria, for such profiling of students to be fair, the nature of the profile should be made clear to students at the start of the course, and assessments should be made and discussed at several points during the course rather than only at the end.

Reference

Mortimore, J. (1984) Profiles in Action. Further Education Unit.

Extracts from a:

TECHNICIAN EDUCATION COUNCIL

Profile Statement for a Course in Technician Studies

Unit: Mathematics 1 (U80/683)

Student:

College:

Date:

Unit General Objectives for the student are that he/she:	Performance NA	3	2	1
A. Arithmetic operations				
1. Evaluates expressions involving integer indices and uses standard form				
2. Evaluates expressions involving negative and fractional indices and relates indices and logarithms				
3. Ensures that answers to numerical problems are reasonable				
4. Understands and uses tables and charts				
5. Performs basic arithmetic operations on a calculator				
B. Algebra				
6. Uses basic notation and rules of algebra				
7. Multiplies and factorises algebraic expressions involving brackets				
8. Solves, algebraically, simple equations and linear simultaneous equations				
9. Evaluates and transforms formulae				
etc.				

NA means not assessed
3 means the student has been assessed but needs more practice
2 means the student has shown basic competence
1 means the student has shown a high degree of competence

General Comments:

Signed: Status:

Hidden Criteria 46

Hidden criteria are those assessment criteria which affect students' grades but which are not made explicit. For example many teachers dislike errors in spelling and punctuation. Teachers often have strong views about length, legibility, colloquial language, badly labelled diagrams, failure to state units of measurement, and so on. They may admit to their colleagues that such factors influence their response to their students' work, but they may not correct them or even comment on them to the students themselves. Even if they do give their students feedback on these issues, the students may not realise the effect they have on marks.

Studies of assessment systems suggest that hidden criteria are widespread, and that they are sometimes quite different from, or even contradictory to, the stated criteria. For example there may be fine-sounding public statements about the importance of creativity and what the individual student can bring to a piece of work, whereas in reality marks may be awarded for following detailed procedures to a prespecified pattern.

Students expect teachers to differ, and many actively look out for clues as to what particular marking foibles each has. If you want to take the guessing out of this process and you want your students to know what your own hidden criteria are:

a write down all those features of student work (eg. bad handwriting) which influence your perception, either positively or negatively;

b hand this list to your students!

Criterion Referenced Assessment 47

Much of the assessment which takes place in education is norm-referenced. This means that the assessment indicates how good one person is in relation to the total group being assessed. A graduate with a first class honours degree in biology, for example, is amongst the top 5 - 10% of graduates. And a student with a grade 'A' in 'A'-level history is amongst the best group of students who took that 'A'-level exam that year. What such assessment systems cannot tell you is what these students know or can do. A biology graduate from one polytechnic will know quite different things from a biology graduate from another polytechnic or from a university, even though they will be of roughly equivalent quality in some general sense. Similarly it is not possible to tell what someone who has passed 'A'-level history can actually do, or which particular aspects of history they would be able to explain. Norm referenced assessment is often used when tough selection decisions have to be made. For example it is common for science laboratory facilities to be insufficient to cope with all first year students continuing into the second and third year of a course. If only 75% of the first year students can be accommodated then 25% have to be failed in their first year exams <u>regardless of how competent they are</u>.

In contrast criterion referenced assessment is concerned with how an individual has performed, quite independently of how others have performed. A clear example of a criterion referenced test is the high jump. There is an absolute cut-off point between 'passing' or 'failing' a 2 metre high jump, the criteria for which are easy to specify and apply, and which have nothing to do with the performance of others. There are quite a number of subject areas in education where criterion referenced assessment would make a lot more sense than the present norm referenced assessment. Instead of being able to say about a course: "Those who have passed this course are amongst the best 80% of their class" it would then be possible to say: "Those who have passed this course can all do the following things: ....".

One such subject area is construction engineering. It is often argued that the reason for the engineering syllabus being so full, and for teaching methods being so teacher dominated, is that there is a certain body of knowledge which all engineers must know "or their bridges will fall down". However in practice the assessment system used is invariably norm-referenced. That is, all it indicates is how good students are in relation to each other. A student with a bare pass on an engineering degree will be amongst the bottom 20% or so of her year in her college. She may also have got half of every question she answered in the final exam wrong. A low pass mark is usually used in order to produce relatively few failures. It is possible to gain recognition as a member of a professional engineering society without being able to do anything at all 100% correctly, simply by avoiding being amongst the bottom group.

This situation would not be tolerated for driving tests. It would clearly not be acceptable if candidates could pass their driving test while staying on the road for only half of the time, or while being able to change gear correctly but not being able to steer. For such assessments there needs to be a set of criteria all of which must be met by the candidate if she is to pass. And there is little sense in producing a mark in such a test. Either the candidate is good enough to be allowed out on the roads on her own or she is not. The driving test is therefore a criterion referenced test. Whether a candidate passes or fails does not depend on how good she is compared with others taking the test at that time, but only on whether she can meet a range of performance criteria.

Such assessment schemes have clear advantages. Students know what constitutes an acceptable learning outcome and they can easily tell when further study is or is not necessary. For employers or others who want information about the abilities of students a criterion referenced sytem of assessment is of particular value because it enables reasonable predictions about what the student will be able to do.

The implementation of criterion referenced assessment is often associated with the use of objectives (see p. 151) and with the use of profiles for reporting learning outcomes (**see 45 Profiles**).

There are two main difficulties associated with criterion referenced assessment:

a it can be difficult to specify criteria even in apparently clear cut subject areas. Even driving testers have to use subjective judgements to decide whether minimum standards have been reached for some criteria such as 'driving at a speed appropriate to traffic conditions';

b many educational systems demand norm referenced assessment outcomes with a spread of marks rather than the pass/fail outcomes of criterion referenced assessment. Teachers who are committed to criterion referenced assessment try to meet these demands by setting large numbers of criteria and then awarding students marks for the number of criteria met (eg. the number of different types of problem which can be solved). They manipulate the distribution of student marks by varying the number of criteria and they set the number of criteria so high that no students ever get 100%. The consequence of fudging the assessment in this way is to produce unreasonably large syllabi, which in turn puts pressure on teachers and students.

Pass/Fail 48

A 'pass/fail' course is one where there is no grading or differentiation amongst those students who pass, but only between those who pass and those who fail. A pass/fail decision is also generally the outcome of criterion referenced assessment (**see 47**) but for different reasons. The main purpose of criterion referenced assessment is to ensure that students who successfully complete a course can do a particular range of things competently; pass/fail courses are usually designed to avoid the negative side effects of assessment rather than to establish performance standards. Such negative side effects can include:

a competitiveness between students when cooperation would lead to more learning. Competitiveness can be especially high in those norm referenced grading systems in which a fixed proportion of students will fail, and in which how well one student does depends partly on how badly others do;

b preoccupation with assessment rather than with learning, leading to a narrowing of interests, cautiousness in the choice of topics or the approach taken to topics, question spotting, and the avoidance of unassessed learning tasks;

c anxiety about performance which inhibits effective studying;

d a heavy workload for lecturers.

Pass/fail assessment is usually introduced onto those courses where it is felt to be especially important for students to explore the subject matter in an open and flexible way without fear of the consequences, and where there are few 'right' answers or defined skills, and few clear performance criteria. Passing is usually defined in terms of fulfilling minimum criteria such as: attendance at classes; submitting assignments; completing a self-assessment form or presenting a seminar paper.

As soon as criteria are phrased in a more limiting way eg. "submitting satisfactory assignments", an element of grading is introduced, and the benefits of the pass/fail system start to be eroded: if students are to produce a 'satisfactory' assignment, this limits their approach to the task and makes them anxious about passing. Conversely pass/fail courses can be ruined by lack of clarity about what constitutes failure, which can both heighten anxiety and increase the likelihood that undisclosed criteria are operating (**see 46 Hidden Criteria**).

Pass/fail courses are quite common in the context of modular or credit accumulation courses where individual short units count towards a final qualification, such as a degree. The assessment pressure in such courses tends to be relentless and pass/fail units are introduced in order to allow students some time to relax and learn for the sake of learning without jeopardising their overall average marks.

Pass/fail elements can also be built in as components of otherwise conventionally assessed courses. Regulations can be framed in the form: "Students must gain an average of 40% on coursework and the exam AND SUBMIT A PROJECT". This can encourage a more adventurous, creative, and therefore risky, approach to the project work than might be the case if it was marked in the same way as other course elements.

Feedback to Students

Teach-Test 49

Teach-test is really a teaching method which is based on assessment. It was developed by Terry Vickers at Trent Polytechnic in the context of science teaching. It centres around having a full test of the crucial elements of a course week by week.

At the end of each week students are given a test on that week's material to work on, in class. The teacher 'tours' the class giving support and advice on request. When common problems are identified, the teacher gives a short impromtu remedial explanation to the whole class. The purpose of the test is not to provide the teacher with information about the students (except in so far as this provides guidance for further teaching) but to provide students with information about their own level of learning so that they can undertake appropriate further study alone.

When the test is completed and outstanding queries have been dealt with, the teacher states the learning objectives for the following week. These indicate what will be addressed in the following week's test. The students are given a handout summarising the following week's work and the teacher briefly indicates the main features of the topic and highlights further reading and references. Student queries are dealt with at this stage but only to clarify what is to be learned. This brief summary is not intended to be a full explanation or a lecture. In fact there is no formal lecture and no other teaching until the test the
following week. Students quickly get used to anticipating the demands of tests and study accordingly, using the feedback they get during tests to guide further study.

The teach-test technique is used most frequently in courses where there is a fixed final exam and no coursework requirement, and where the subject matter lends itself to the clear specification of objectives and the easy testing of knowledge. The effectiveness of the technique for preparing students for final exams has been well demonstrated.

A booklet and a 35 minute videotape describing the method in detail, and demonstrating the method in action, including students' reactions to the method, are available from:

Central A.V. Services,
Trent Polytechnic,
Burton Street,
Nottingham NG1 4BU.

Reference

Vickers, T. 1984 The Teach-Test Technique Standing Conference for Educational Development Services in Polytechnics. Joint Publication No.1. Birmingham.

SAQs 50

The acronym SAQ first became widely known through its use by the Open University in their printed learning materials. It stands for Self Assessment Question. In Open University course materials you will find SAQs used extensively: interspersed though the text and collected together in clusters at the end of sections and booklets. Their purpose is primarily to provide a device through which students can engage in an active thoughtful way with the material instead of simply reading it passively. SAQs may require the student to give a written response, check through a previous section, interpret a set of data, read sections from other books, or simply give the topic some quiet thought before progressing to the next section. Answers are given to provide feedback, sometimes immediately after the question, but more usually at the end of the booklet. The answers allow students to check whether they are on the right track, and may include remedial advice or refer the student to the section of the booklet or other books where the basis for the answer can be found. The answers come in a variety of forms such as checklists, model answers, discussions and so on.

There is no involvement of the teacher in this questioning and answering. SAQs are designed for students to use on their own- and they do this in a bewildering variety of ways, including looking up the answer and then trying to work out the relationship between it and the question. Although designed for use in distance-learning material, the idea of offering questions <u>and answers</u> for students to use in their private study can equally well be used in other areas of education. To some extent the kinds of problem sheets commonly used in science and technology are like SAQs except that answers are usually given out at a later date rather than being available to students along with the questions to use as they see fit.

Possible applications of SAQs might be:

a lecture handouts with SAQs to encourage subsequent thought about the lecture;

b reading lists with SAQs for each topic or book to give feedback on private reading;

c SAQs on an overhead projector transparency at the start of a lecture, as students settle down, with the answers provided on a second OHP before the lecture starts;

d sets of SAQs on special handouts for each section of a course.

By offering SAQs you will be identifying for students what you consider to be important issues on the course, and your answers will enable them to judge whether they are giving enough attention to these issues.

Feedback Classroom 51

A feedback classroom is one where arrangements have been made to give the teacher immediate feedback on what students have learned and understood, so that teaching can be adjusted accordingly. Students are asked test questions, not to assess them or to give students feedback (though both of these are possible additional benefits of feedback classrooms), but to inform the teacher about the consequences of her teaching as she goes along.

It is clearly possible simply to ask students a question and then go round getting everyone's answer. However this would be slow, and students might be reluctant to answer and liable to repeat the answers of those who spoke before them. Instead you could ask students to answer by saying:

> "Those who think this is the answer, please put your hand up...... Now those who think this is the answer, please put your hand up...."

This would take less time but would still be clumsy and students would still be able to copy others' answers rather than thinking for themselves, and so give a distorted impression of what the whole class understood.

A simple solution is provided by the Cosford Cube. This is a small cube with each face coloured differently. One is held by each student. When a question is asked, the possible answers are 'colour coded' by the teacher eg. red for no, green for yes, or different colours for multiple choice answers. (These can be displayed on an overhead projection transparency.) Students simply select the colour which indicates their choice of answer and point that face of their cube towards the teacher. The teacher can see at a glance whether the right colour is pointed towards her, or which wrong colour is pointed most frequently. She can also identify which students have got the correct answer, and which students regularly get it wrong. At the same time students cannot easily see what answers other students are giving and have to think for themselves.

At Brunel Technical College they used to have an electronic classroom. In front of each seat in a tiered lecture theatre was a row of labelled buttons. Teachers coded possible answers to questions in terms of these button labels and students responded by pressing the appropriate button. Their responses were counted electronically and displayed on an electronic screen for both students and the lecturer to see. Current American versions of the same system use hand-held, infra-red, cordless response panels with numbered buttons. Students punch in their answers and point their controls at a large TV screen which displays pooled responses in the form of bar charts for all to see. As well as giving feedback to the teachers, these systems give immediate feedback to the students about their colleagues' responses.

Student Requests For Feedback 52

Writing comments on students' work is a time-consuming part of a teacher's job and can be very discouraging: often there seems to be little evidence that students have taken the feedback seriously or even, at times, understood it.

One way of ensuring that students pay more attention to your feedback, and that it will be seen to answer their needs directly, is to ask them what kind of feedback they want. If it is what they have asked for, they will be motivated to take it seriously. They are in the best position to know what their difficulties are and to judge what kind of feedback is helpful.

Students' requests for feedback can be elicited from individuals or from the group as a whole.

If you want requests from individual students, you can ask them when they do a piece of assessed writing to add a note at the end specifying what kind of feedback they would like. (You can include this in a handout of your assignment titles.) Your students will probably need some encouragement the first time and an explanation of why you think it's a good idea and maybe some examples of the kind of requests they might make.

When invited to choose, some students just ask for general comments but given the opportunity most students find it easy to identify areas where they have difficulty, and ask specific questions such as: "I'm not sure if I have answered the question. Have I?" Often they write at some length.

Here are some examples of requests for feedback from students on an English literature course:

> "nb Sue - could you give this the full treatment, pointing out spelling mistakes, grammatical errors etc. And Sue, just one thing - be kind."

> "Dear Sue
> Please ignore my spelling and typing errors as i think they are totaly irrelivant to the arguements I am trying to put across. Apart from this please feel free, and I would like to invite you to criticise my work on every point that you think is relivant. The more criticism I get on the essay the more I can put right in the next."

> "Sue, could you let me know your opinion on my style, as well as the actual content. Don't worry about spelling unless its really awful!"

> "I think I have expressed myself clumsily in this analysis - especially in terms of the way my sentences are organised or disorganised. The kind of feedback I would like is (a) to see whether you think it is disjointed, and (b) for you to show me how you go about doing this type of exercise."

These students clearly wanted rather different kinds of feedback, and what suited one would have annoyed another.

If you want a request from the whole group, you can set up a pyramid exercise to enable students to clarify and pool their ideas. Pyramid exercises operate in four stages: first, students work on their own, then in pairs, then in fours, and finally as a total group. You could say:

Stage 1

"I'd like you to spend five minutes looking through the comments on your marked essays from the course so far."

Stage 2

"Now, in pairs, give each other examples of good feedback and bad feeedback. Take five minutes to talk about this."

Stage 3

"Now get into fours and draw up a list of guidelines for feedback which I can use as a checklist when I am marking your work. Use examples from your marked work, or use your own ideas, or both. One member of the group act as scribe andwrite down the list. You've got fifteen minutes for this."

Stage 4

"Now I'd like the scribe from each group in turn to read out that group's list and I'll make a total list on the blackboard. When we've got the whole list written up, we'll see if any points are duplicated or if there are any which present problems. What we are working towards is a list which you and I can all agree to. O.K. can we start with the scribe from this group?"

(See also **53 Feedback Checklists** which was drawn up by a group of students using this pyramid exercise.)

If students are asked what kind of feedback they want, not only are they more likely to receive it but in specifying it they are getting practice at self assessment. It is also better for their self respect if they identify their strengths and weaknesses themselves. An additional benefit is that their requests often constitute feedback to the teacher about her usual methods. For example, a student may say: "Please try to give me constructive criticism and not just praise" or "Please try to find a kinder way of telling me when I misunderstand things".

Feedback Checklists 53

A feedback checklist is a set of guidelines for giving feedback to students. Teachers can use a feedback checklist to evaluate the quality of their own written comments on students' work.

Such a checklist can be devised and administered by the head of deartment, or course tutor. The Open University, for example, operates a checklist system whereby staff tutors (who supervise the tutors who mark students' work) evaluate a sample of each tutor's marking against a checklist which includes such items as the balance between single word and full sentence comments, and the balance between positive and negative comments..

The checklist does not have to be imposed from above, however. Members of a course team can devise and administer their own. The items in such a list could arise out of discussions following a staff marking exercise (**see 44**).

Alternatively individual teachers can make their own lists, in consultation with their students. On page 176 is a checklist which was drawn up by a group of Further Education Teaching Certificate students at Bristol Polytechnic, using the kind of pyramid discussion exercise described in: **52 Student Requests for Feedback.**

GUIDELINES FOR GIVING FEEDBACK

1. Keep the time short between the student writing and the feedback
2. Where possible give instantaneous feedback
3. Tie in the grade with the comment (i.e. not "An excellent piece of work: D")
4. Summarise the comments and flag the fact that it's a summary
5. Balance positive with negative
6. Flag what is positive and what is negative
7. Negative points should be constructive
8. Indicate how the student can improve
9. Follow up with oral feedback
10. Aim for a dialogue
11. Encourage students to evaluate themselves
12. Encourage students to ask for feedback elsewhere (e.g. from other students or other members of staff)
13. Ask students what kind of feedback they want
14. Make the criteria clear when setting the work and relate the feedback to the criteria
15. Distinguish between different skills (e.g. the student may have lots of good ideas but be poor at spelling)
16. Offer help (e.g. "Would you like a refresher course on the use of the apostrophe?")
17. Give affective feedback (e.g. "It's really frustrating reading your essay because it could have been good but..." or "I enjoyed reading this...")
18. Make further suggestions (e.g. for further reading or developing ideas)
19. Distinguish between formative and summative assessments
20. Give periodic oral feedback on rough drafts

VOLUME 13, NUMBER 1
MARCH 1988

Studies in Higher Education

This international journal, published under the auspices of the Society for Research into Higher Education, expanded from two to three issues a year in 1985. While it is ready to publish worthwhile articles on any aspect of higher education, pride of place is given to those which throw light on the day-to-day processes of teaching and learning and the social and institutional contexts in which they take place. The central aim is to bring together subject specialists from a wide variety of fields in the discussion of teaching issues.

The journal is published three times a year, in March, June and October.
These three annual issues constitute one volume. An annual index and title-page is bound in the October issue.
Volume 13–1988 ISSN 0307-5079

INTERESTING WAYS TO TEACH

No 1. 53 INTERESTING THINGS TO DO IN YOUR LECTURES

Graham Gibbs Sue Habeshaw Trevor Habeshaw

53 practical ideas in 8 Chapters:

Structuring The Process
Using Handouts
Structuring And Summarising Content
Active Learning During Lectures
Improving Students' Notes
Linking Lectures
Holding Attention
Checking On Learning

No 2. 53 INTERESTING THINGS TO DO IN YOUR SEMINARS AND TUTORIALS

Sue Habeshaw Trevor Habeshaw Graham Gibbs

53 practical ideas in 8 Chapters :

Starting Off
Encouraging Students To Participate
Encouraging Students To Take Responsibility
Evaluating The Work Of The Group
Student-Led Seminars
Group Work
Written Material
Expressing Feelings

No 3 53 INTERESTING WAYS TO ASSESS YOUR STUDENTS

Graham Gibbs Sue Habeshaw Trevor Habeshaw

53 practical ideas in 7 Chapters:

Essays
Alternative Exams
Assessing Practical And Project Work
Giving Feedback To Students
Objective Tests
Computer-Based Assessment
Criteria

No 4 53 INTERESTING WAYS OF HELPING YOUR STUDENTS TO STUDY

Trevor Habeshaw Graham Gibbs Sue Habeshaw

53 practical ideas in 7 Chapters:

Beginning
Reading
Learning With Others
Revision And Exams
Planning
Writing And Note-Taking
Using The Library

No 5 53 INTERESTING COMMUNICATION EXERCISES FOR SCIENCE STUDENTS

Di Steeds Sue Habeshaw

53 practical ideas in 13 Chapters:

Communication Theory
Study Skills
The Language Of Science
Writing Up Practicals
Writing Instructions
Table Exercises
Self Presentation
Thinking About Science
Using The Library
Technical Writing
Report Writing
Data Presentation And Interpretation
Oral Presentations

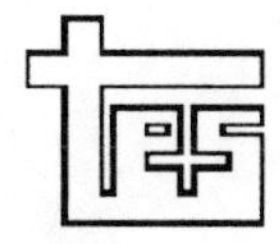

TECHNICAL AND EDUCATIONAL SERVICES

ORDER FORM

(NB These prices are subject to change without notice. If in doubt please check with us before ordering.)

Please supply :	No. of copies	£
53 Interesting Things to Do in Your Lectures (£7 UK, £10 airmail)	......	.....
53 Interesting Things to Do in Your Seminars and Tutorials (£7 UK, £10 airmail)	......	.....
53 Interesting Ways to Assess Your Students (£7 UK, £10 airmail)	......	.....
53 Interesting Communication Exercises for Science Students (£8UK, £11airnail)	......	.....
53 Interesting Ways of Helping Your Students to Study (£8UK, £11airnail)	......	.....
53 Interesting Ways to Appraise Your Teaching (£8 UK, £11 airmail)	......	.....
253 Ideas for your teaching (£7 UK, £10 airmail)	......	.....
Interesting Ways To Teach: 7 'Do-it-yourself' Exercises (£7 UK, £10 airmail)	......	.....
Creating a Teaching Profile (£6 UK, £9 airmail)	......	.....
Total	**£**	

Book prices (January1989) include p&p. U.K. and overseas surface mail. Books are sent airmail by request at a charge of £3 sterling per book. A banker's commission of £3.50 should be added to invoices to be settled in currencies other than £ sterling. Discount 10% on 10 or more books.

All orders and invoices to
Technical and Educational Services Ltd, 37 Ravenswood Road, Bristol BS6 6BW UK.
Ansaphone (0272) 245446
Please make cheques payable to **'Technical and Educational Services Ltd'.**

Technical and Educational Services Ltd reserve the right to change prices at any time without notice.

Name

....

Address

....

....